UNITED IN HIS NAME

Theology and Life Series

2

UNITED IN HIS NAME

Jesus in Our Midst
in the experience and thought of
Chiara Lubich

Judith M. Povilus

with a Preface by
Bishop Robert F. Morneau

New City Press

Published in the United States by New City Press
86 Mayflower Avenue, New Rochelle, New York 10801
©1992 New City Press, New York

Translated by Jerry Hearne from the original Italian edition
«Gesú in Mezzo» nel pensiero di Chiara Lubich
©1981 Città Nuova Editrice, Rome, Italy

Cover design by Nick Cianfarani

Library of Congress Cataloging-in-Publication Data:

Povilus, Judith M.
    [Gesú in mezzo nel pensiero di Chiara Lubich.   English]
    United in his name : Jesus in our midst in the experience and
    thought of Chiara Lubich /   Judith M. Povilus.
        p.   cm.   —   (Theology and life series ; v. 2)
    Includes bibliographical references.
    ISBN 1-56548-003-1 : $8.95
    1. Spiritual life—Christianity—History of doctrines—20th
    century.   2. Jesus Christ—History of doctrines—20th century.
    3. Lubich, Chiara, 1920-.   4. Focolare Movement.   I. Title.
    II. Series.
    BX2350.2.P6313   1992
    232—dc20   92-20690

Unless otherwise indicated, scriptural quotations are from
The New American Bible
©1970 Confraternity of Christian Doctrine

Printed in the United States of America

CONTENTS

PREFACE

The American essayist Ralph Waldo Emerson once commented: "A new person is to me a great event and hinders me from sleep."

Several years ago I met Chiara Lubich through her writings. A line from her *Unity and Jesus Forsaken* has stayed with me for more than five years: "Looking at him [Jesus forsaken], every renunciation is possible."[1] Here is the pivotal point of the spirituality that characterizes the Focolare movement: Jesus in our midst; the presence of God that is continuous, warm, silent, fruitful, luminous; a way of life that judges all in terms of love and unity. I haven't slept well, much to my benefit (surprisingly), since encountering this unambiguous and challenging spirituality.

The scripture scholar Walter Brueggemann lists six major crises that impact on our world today: isolation and alienation; the failure of the community to care; the dispute between those who have and those who lack the necessities of life; civil strife that destroys millions of lives; the erosion of images and symbols that heal and unite us; an insatiable consumerism that cheapens life. This is the social and political context facing the disciple of Christ and the community we call Church. What values do we bring to these horrendous problems that thwart the coming of God's kingdom?

The Focolare movement is concerned about unity. Well aware of the loneliness, isolation and alienation that many experience, the Focolare spirituality stresses the primacy of unity. Its primary mode of seeing is that of oneness. What overcomes division is the power of Jesus living in our midst. Bondedness with Christ makes peace possible. "May they all be one" is the refrain that provides meaning and direction to this spirituality. In his work *Contemporary Theologians,* James J. Bacik summaries an insight from the great theologian Ives Congar that deals with the crisis of isolation:

> The unity we seek is found, not in a dull uniformity or in rigid doctrinal formulas, but in the rich and diverse life of the church members who are committed to Christ in faith. Unity is not the victory of one denomination over others, but

the victory of Christ, who prayed that his followers might be one.[2]

Individualism is a strong force in our times. When the primary language is the "I" and not the "We," communities fail to care and thereby neglect to foster the common good. Chiara Lubich stresses community as a central theme in her attempt to live the gospel. Community involves reciprocal love. Mutuality characterizes the Focolarini way of life. Again it is Jesus who holds the community together. His presence must never be forgotten. This concept of community is grounded in the very nature of the Trinity. A triune God shares divine life with the created world calling us to care for one another in a manner similar to the inner dynamics of the trinitarian life. A noble calling. Ruth Burrows, a spiritual writer, reminds us: "Community does not just happen, it has to be worked for, whether it be the community of the family or any community whatsoever. A community is not just a group living together. It is persons in communion and can never be built except on self-sacrifice."[3]

Of special concern to the Focolare community are those who are deprived—who lack a sense of dignity, physical goods, love, forgiveness. Chiara raises the question about the suffering of Jesus: "Are not the anguished, the lonely, the disheartened, the disillusioned, the fallen, the weak. . .similar to him?" Not only is the central verse "Where two or three are gathered in my name. . ." (Mt 18, 20) prominent in this spirituality but also "I assure you, as often as you did it for one of my least brothers, you did it for me" (Mt 25, 40). Jesus is present in every person and circumstance. We are to respond to the poor just as we would respond to the person of Jesus, living in them as he is living with us. "You will have found Christ when you are concerned with other people's sufferings and not your own,"[4] says Flannery O'Connor.

A fourth major crisis in our times: civil strife. We see this in war-torn countries, on our city streets, in our homes, indeed, within our hearts. Daily thousands upon thousands of people experience violence, many death. The darkness of hatred and sheer ignorance lead to the destruction of innocent lives. In the face of this darkness a light shines, indeed a fire of truth and a burning light of love. The truth is that God wills peace for all in and through Jesus. The love of God's Spirit empowers us to be agents of reconciliation and peacemakers in a fragile and broken world.

What does the Focolare movement have to say regarding the erosion of images and symbols that hold a community together, that heal and unite us by recalling our stories and singing our songs? The large symbol is the cross! The overwhelming mystery: Jesus forsaken! Because Jesus was obedient to the cross, redemption came into the world. There is no other image or symbol that has such driving force nor any other image that is so threatening to a world seeking to avoid suffering at all cost. The cross is the symbol of God's love; the cross reunites us to God through the redemptive obedience of our Lord. We must meditate on the mystery of the cross daily. This insight from Fr. John Shea may be helpful:

> The Cross is the communication of God's care but it is not a message from the outside. God loves us by receiving our lives into himself as we experience them—torn and broken. The Cross is God loving us from inside. God has accepted those aspects of our lives we ourselves have disowned and denied. We fight the awareness of our guilt, proving ourselves innocent at all costs. We fear suffering and death so fiercely that it dominates our imaginations and dictates to us the shape of our days. If Creation is God's presence to our beauty, the Cross is God's presence to our pain and twistedness.[5]

Again, unity and love and the presence of God. Jesus in our midst in joy and sorrow, in light and darkness, in victory and defeat.

A final crisis that the spiritual vision of Chiara Lubich addresses: the insatiable consumerism that is destroying and cheapening all human life. When love and the presence of Jesus is at the center of one's consciousness then "things" find their proper place. An ordering comes into life that allows us to be free. Idolatry is rejected. Simplicity and self-forgetfulness become a way of life. A willing renunciation of everything that is an obstacle to unity is embraced with joy. A festive atmosphere is experienced in Focolare communities because true poverty of spirit lights up every face. A refusal to be entrapped by things creates space within the heart for the lodging of the Lord and his poor.

A contemporary poet, Jessica Powers, in reflecting on Christ as our utmost need, captures well the core dimension of Focolare spirituality. This prayer/poem is a good introduction and conclusion to the writing of Chiara Lubich.

> Late, late the mind confesses:
> wisdom has not sufficed.
> I cannot take one step into the light
> without the Christ.
>
> Late, late the heart affirmed:
> wild do my heart-beats run
> when in the blood-stream sings one wish away
> from the Incarnate Son.
>
> Christ is my utmost need.
> I lift each breath, each beat for Him to bless,
> knowing our language cannot overspeak
> our frightening helplessness.
>
> Here where proud morning walks
> and we hang wreaths on power and self-command,
> I cling with all my strength unto a nail-
> investigated hand.
>
> Christ is my only trust.
> I am my fear since, down the lanes of ill,
> my steps surprised a dark Iscariot
> plotting in my own will.
>
> Past nature called, I cry
> who clutch at fingers and at tunic folds,
> "Lay not on me, O Christ, this fastening.
> Yours be the hand that holds."[6]

Robert F. Morneau
Auxiliary Bishop of Green Bay

INTRODUCTION

A. INTRODUCTORY NOTES

Chiara Lubich and the Focolare movement she has founded stand out as figures of our time, both within and outside of Church circles.[1] The contribution they have brought is one of spirit and life, underlined on numerous occasions by Pope Paul VI[2] and Pope John Paul II.

It is not the purpose of this research, however, to present the person of Chiara Lubich, nor to study the origins and developments, or evaluate the impact of the Focolare itself.[3]

As the title indicates, our study focuses on a specific theme—the theme of Jesus in our midst—in the thought of Chiara Lubich. This is one of the principal ideas forming the basis of the spirituality of the movement that grew around her.[4] It refers to the presence of the Risen Christ in the collectivity which he himself had promised in verse 20 of the 18th chapter of Matthew: "Where two or three are gathered together in my name, there am I in the midst of them."[5]

This study is of a spiritual-dogmatic nature. Chiara, in fact, does not present herself as a theologian, but rather as one who bears a spirituality that many have confirmed to contain a charism. While engrafting itself into the long tradition of theological thought, the spirituality also brings into light new and timely intuitions, as we shall see.

The sources for this work are published writings, unedited writings, and recorded conversations and talks later put into written form. In regard to the recordings, with Chiara's permission small literary alterations were made in cases where the written form proved more conducive. The text will indicate which talks were already prepared in written form beforehand.

Though we acknowledge the novelty in the use of tape recordings as a source for a scientific study, we do feel it is justifiable inasmuch as it permits us to present Chiara's thought from the viewpoints of its many nuances.

11

In general, we opted for completeness over conciseness, risking repetition, so as to organize and render accessible to as many readers as possible the vast array of material that treats a topic that is so new and meaningful for our times.

Since everything began through an experience of life, which then led to a period of intellectual illuminations, we will often find ourselves, especially when concerned with the illuminative period, in areas where spiritual theology and mysticism cross the more rigid schematics of reasoning. We will see however that Chiara herself will elaborate on many of her ideas, expressing them in more accessible terms and confronting them with the thought of others, above all with the Fathers of the Church.

The development of this presentation appears to us well founded. In fact, Christianity itself began through an experience of life: the experience that many in the early Christian communities made of Christ and of new life in him ("What we have heard, what we have seen with our eyes, what we have looked upon and our hands have touched" [1 Jn 1:1-3]). Over time the contents of this experience were examined, developed, ordered and conclusions were drawn. Therefore, this movement from life to doctrine is inherent to Christianity.

Affirming that an experience of life can bring a valid contribution to theology, *The Dogmatic Constitution on Divine Revelation* of Vatican II states:

> This Tradition that comes from the apostles makes progress in the Church, with the help of the Holy Spirit. There is a growth in insight into the realities and words that are being passed on. This comes about in various ways. It comes through the contemplation and study of believers who ponder these things in their hearts (cf. Lk 2:19 and 51). It comes from the intimate sense of spiritual realities which they experience. And it comes from the preaching of those who have received, along with their right of succession in the episcopate, the sure charism of truth. Thus, as the centuries go by, the Church is always advancing towards the plenitude of divine truth, until eventually the words of God are fulfilled in her.[6]

Back to our theme, we repeat that it is only today that the topic of Jesus in our midst begins to unfold again in the ambit of the Catholic Church, particularly in pastoral spheres, after years of near silence about this reality. From what we have been able to examine, to this date there do not exist any further studies as such. For articles relevant to the theme, one can consult the bibliography of an essay of mine mentioned in the preface. Besides this one, and also within the context of the Focolare, there is an exegetical study by Gerard Rosse on the passage of Matthew 18:20[7] and a pastoral essay by the German bishop and theologian Klaus Hemmerle.[8] The latter has also written the preface to Chiara's book *Jesus in Our Midst*, underlining the theme's theological value.

B. THE GENESIS OF THE THEME OF JESUS IN OUR MIDST IN THE THOUGHT OF CHIARA LUBICH

"Where two or three are gathered together in my name, there am I in the midst of them" (Mt 18:20).

These words come from the gospel of Matthew, written almost two thousand years ago. Nevertheless, along the course of Church history after the patristic era, they have hardly been given mention. How did Chiara come to understand them in such a complete way, and even draw from them such a rich spirituality?

If we look back to the beginning of the Focolare, we see through Chiara's account that the heart of the theme we want to treat, that is, the very reality of what Jesus has promised in his words "Where two or three are gathered together in my name there am I in the midst of them," is the fruit of a vital experience.[9]

The first step in this experience was to understand that the new commandment of Jesus, "Love one another as I have loved you" (Jn 13:34), needed be lived to the letter. The word "as" demanded from each person a total love for the other—*caritas*; each person was to be ready to sacrifice oneself for the other, to be consumed in one (cf. Jn 17:23) with the other, to die for the other.

Chiara, through the grace of God, began to live in this way with her companions, and they experienced that their lives took on a "leap in quality."[10] Each sensed a peace, a light, and a supernatural joy never before experienced, which included fruits of conversion unproportional to their own human efforts.

Afterward, when reading the words of Matthew 18:20, Chiara understood that they explained the new reality that she was experiencing with her companions: the presence of Jesus himself as he had promised. Years later, when explaining how it happened, Chiara explains: "I discovered him [Jesus in their midst] because he was there. In loving one another, we had established his presence . . . he enlightened us, he led us to understand the gospel. We understood the words of the gospel 'where two or three are united, I am there,' that is, it was he who revealed himself."[11] Therefore, at the core there lies an existing and ongoing experience, followed by an enlightenment on the depth of the reality being lived: an enlightenment which Chiara attributed to the same presence of Jesus in their midst which they were already living with, though not fully understanding what it was.

In the various accounts of the beginnings of the Focolare told by Chiara, one always finds this fundamental sequence. What came first was not a reflection on the meaning of Matthew 18:20, followed then by the effort to put it into practice. It happened the other way around. A reality was first lived, or experienced, and its explanation was discovered afterward as a consequence.[12]

The exact date of this "discovery" in Chiara's experience is not known. The first time a clear reference to this concept appears in her writings goes back to January 1945. A letter of that period makes an initial mention of the presence of God among many in relation to reciprocal love and unity, although the text does not seem to focus as of yet, on the passage of Matthew 18:20; at least not specifically. In the letter Chiara speaks of a "love of God and of neighbor to the extent of being consumed in unity," and also of "the will of God which is reciprocal love—the new commandment—the pearl of the gospel!" She continues to affirm that in living this commandment, through a choice of the cross, "you will work toward fusing your little community into a solid block and thus give the greatest glory to God! Then God will live among you. You will sense it, you will enjoy his presence; he will give you his light; he will enflame you with his love."[13]

14

Thus, we find the following elements: reciprocal love, unity, the community, the presence of God "among" many made tangible by the light and fire of love.

Unity was spoken about even before this particular date. Chiara recalled, years later, a day in 1944, when Trent was under an air attack. As she and her companions were huddled inside an underground shelter, they read the passage of John 17:11 "Father, may they all be one," and felt the call to live for its fulfillment.[14]

In another letter dated around the same period, we find the initial idea of this call:

> Let's love one another! One day we will find ourselves all united up there for all eternity, if down here we would have had the courage to love one another without reserve— united in a common ideal: universal brotherhood, in one Father, God who is in heaven.[15]

There exists a writing entitled "Unity," dated November 2 and 12, 1946, in which the concept of unity is greatly detailed, and which contains a word on the presence of God "among two souls who are fused in unity." Clear is the idea that the presence of Jesus is the result of unity, though the specific term "Jesus in our midst" is not yet used, nor is there any reference to Matthew 18:20. For now, we will present just a few of its passages.

> Only Christ can make two into one; it is because his love is the emptying of self, it is "non egoism," which allows us to reach the depths of others' hearts. To love. I in you and you in me.

> Love our neighbors as ourselves. This happens only when the two are one; the first makes oneself the other, and the second does the same.

> The important thing is to keep aflame, vibrant, and most ardent the current of love and peace that circulates among us. We must aim at making it penetrate always more among those who live around us.[16]

> What does the combination of two or more souls form? Jesus—Oneness.

> No one gives greater glory to God than God himself and God is present in a person who empties oneself in order to

allow Christ to relive in him or her, and in Christ, the Father—and when two souls are fused (through a reciprocal, loving, forgetting of self, the result of a heroic humility and an ardent love) they give prominence to Christ.

When unity makes its way, it leaves just one mark: Christ.[17]

Besides being a very profound explanation of unity, we note in this passage that Christ is the one who forms unity (giving us true love) and that he is the result of unity: Jesus remains present in the mutual cancelation of our egos. We note all the dynamism involved: Chiara speaks of a current that is vibrant, aflame, and ardent.

The first specific reference to Matthew 18:20 appears in a short letter dated September 6, 1947. It is evident that Chiara discovers how this sentence of the New Testament fully explains what she had already experienced and clearly described. In this letter, speaking of Mary who wants us united, Chiara says:

She knows that "where two or more" are united in the holy name of her Son, he is in their midst!

And where Jesus is present, dangers disperse, obstacles vanish. . . . He overcomes all things, because he is love![18]

We note the objective reality of this concept of Jesus' presence. Because he is truly present, there are tangible consequences: difficulties are overcome.

Then in January 1948 an article appeared in the *Amico Serafico*, an Italian magazine of the Third Order of Franciscans and the African Missionaries (Mozambique) of the Capuchin Fathers of Trent. It contained this paragraph:

Jesus will return in the midst of Catholic Christians because to speak of Jesus means to speak of brotherhood: meaning "I give you a new commandment; love one another as I have loved you," and "where two or more are gathered together in my name, there am I in the midst of them." Jesus, having been made the bond of Christians, will resolve all social problems in charity and in truth. . . . Let's unite with one another. Our strength lies in unity, because the unity we speak of is Jesus.[19]

The next issue carried a continuation of the same article:

Let us be united with one another in truth and in charity. In small numbers first, let us live out Christ's most ardent desire: "That they may be one." Made one as much as possible with him and among ourselves, we will fulfill every hidden desire of social justice. We will give to the world and to heaven itself the spectacle, perhaps never seen before, of a small kingdom of God, a kingdom of love. Built amidst toil and sorrow on earth, it will see its triumph in heaven.[20]

The emphasis in these articles does not center on Jesus in our midst. However, when mentioned, several elements emerge surprisingly clear: the link between Matthew 18:20 and John 13:34; Jesus, the "bond of Christians"; and the intuition that even social problems will find their solutions in Jesus. We find in this text the desire to fulfill the passage "that all may be one," along with a prophetic, eschatological vision of the kingdom that already begins here in order to come to completion in heaven.

Various letters from the following months contain so clear a reference to Jesus among us, that they reveal how deeply this key idea had taken root. We quote just a few lines.[21]

In a letter of February 27, 1948, Chiara states:

What a joy it is to know that Jesus—our only treasure and wisdom, our only joy and source of life (of the life we are fond of) is among them, as he is among us! They are not lacking anything now! . . .

Therefore: before all else (even though in this *all* there may be the most beautiful and sacred things like prayer, celebrating Mass, etc.), may we be one! If this occurs, it would no longer be they who act, pray and celebrate . . . but *Jesus in them!*[22]

We note the great value given to the presence of Jesus in our midst and the affirmation that Jesus in our midst guarantees the presence of Jesus in each one.

Here are a few lines from a letter written in April of that same year:

Have no fear of anything whatsoever. Fear only to become attached to something other than to *Jesus among you*. This

17

is your and our ideal. *Jesus among you* (which brings you among us) is also the guarantee of *Jesus in you* in the fullness of unity with him![23]

At the end of the same month, Chiara forcefully speaks about "Jesus among us," drawing a link to unity:

> Unity . . . who could dare speak about it?
> It is as ineffable as God.
> You can sense it, see it, enjoy it; but it is ineffable!
> All enjoy its presence, all suffer its absence.
> It is peace, joy, love, ardor, an atmosphere of heroism and unlimited generosity.
> It is Jesus among us!
> Jesus among us! To live so as to have him always with us! So as to be always creating him (understand me well) among us. So as to bring him to a world so unaware of his peace, so as to carry his light in us! . . .
>
> I would want the whole world to collapse, save but him among us, among us united in his name, because we are dead to our own![24]

Here is a clear identification of Jesus in our midst with unity and a description of how tangible a reality it is through the effects it produces. We also note the fundamental importance given to this presence of his ("the whole world to collapse . . .") and the implication that each must do one's own part to "create him" (Jesus among us) and keep him always. Expressed also is the idea that this reality does not remain something to be enjoyed in closed circles, but becomes a gift for the entire world.

In the space of only a year since the first clear mention of Matthew 18:20, the idea became so vivid as to be developed in an article written by Chiara and published by Igino Giordani[25] in the October 1948 edition of the Italian magazine *Fides*. With this it became a fundamental part of the history of the newborn movement.

> We clearly understood that everything lies in love, that reciprocal love had to be the final teaching of Jesus to his followers, that being "consumed in one" could have been the

only last prayer of Jesus to the Father—the deepest synthesis of the Good News. . . .

To consume ourselves in one: it was our life's program so as to be able to love him.

But where two or three are united in his name, he is in their midst.

Each time unity triumphed over our nature's resistance to die, we felt his divine presence: the presence of his light, his love, his strength.

Jesus among us.

The first little fraternal society, his true disciples, was formed.

Jesus, the bond of unity.

Jesus, king of each single heart, for the life of unity presupposes the complete death of the ego.

Jesus, king of this small group of souls.[26]

At this point, the concept of Jesus in our midst has been born!

We now pass on to a systematic presentation of the theme itself, and its relation to other fundamental themes. We will break it down as such:

1. What is Jesus in our midst and how can one be part of this reality (its conditions and effects).
2. The depth of this reality (the life of unity and its trinitarian dimension; Jesus in our midst and the Holy Spirit; Jesus in our midst and *Jesus forsaken*).
3. Ecclesial aspects and the renewal of society.
4. Jesus in our midst and the Work of Mary.

For clarity's sake, we will not necessarily hold to a chronological sequence of the cited texts. Initially, we will give a general historical background that will help in the understanding of the language Chiara used throughout the years and in placing her various writings into the context of her life.

We already mentioned that the understanding of Jesus in our midst grew out of an existential experience: a specific way of living paved the way to grasping the meaning of the words of Matthew

19

18:20. This holds true for the initial period (1943–48) as well as for afterward. The years 1949–51 introduce a new and characteristic element in Chiara's experience. A series of enlightenments or intellectual visions provide for Chiara a confirmation and new depth to the spirituality that step by step had developed. Chiara communicated her intuitions to her companions and at times put them into writing. This particular wave of light explains the language used and the often contemplative and mystical tone evident in the writings of this period, which reveal also a particular depth. We can say that the heart of Chiara's thought on Jesus in our midst is already entirely contained in the two previous periods, but reaches here its contemplative peak.

The years to follow bring a different tone to her writings on Jesus in our midst: a more "pastoral" one, if we can say so. Superiors counseled a certain caution in the language to adopt.[27] At the same time, the growing circle of people from every age and societal level who wished to live with Jesus in their midst opened a need for a detailed, understandable and organically written explanation on this point, as well as on all of the other points of the spirituality. In 1959, on occasion of the summer Mariapolis meeting, Chiara prepared such a synthesis, parts of it written, parts of it on tape,[28] including the point on Jesus in our midst. It was the first attempt to construct a comprehensive treatise on this theme.

In the same year, an article entitled "Gesú in mezzo" (Jesus in our midst) appeared in *Città Nuova* [the Italian edition of *Living City*], the magazine of the Focolare, presenting a portion of this synthesis.[29] And then in 1965 the brochure "The Focolare Movement" dedicated a chapter on the same topic.[30] In addition, new questions and perspectives arose concerning the implementation of this theme in the most varied aspects of life, which Chiara then deepens and explains, often through talks given during meetings of the Focolare. These talks have been recorded for the use of the Focolare's members and to some degree have also been published. The language adopted in these cases is at times informal, but the existence of outlines and Chiara's hand-written notes indicate to us that the main points have been prepared and thought through beforehand.

Finally, we note something new in Chiara's writings during the last decade treated in this book (1965–75). While continuing to develop her pastoral presentation of this theme, we see more and more that she accompanies it with quotations from Fathers of the Church, the Second Vatican Council, popes, and various theologians and saints. This is especially true in her book *Jesus in Our Midst*, published in 1976, in which she extensively quotes the Fathers of the Church.

It would be important to keep in mind that the theme of Jesus in our midst is only one of the various aspects of Chiara's spirituality, which—as was said—bears a charism. This explains the often strong and seemingly prophetic tone which emerges in many of her writings.

Bearing in mind these elements, and the development itself in Chiara's own writing form and expression, we move on to present the thought of Chiara on Jesus in our midst.

Chapter 1

WHAT IS THE PRESENCE OF JESUS IN OUR MIDST AND HOW CAN WE PARTAKE IN IT?

As we can see from Chiara's writings, Jesus in the midst is one of the various forms of a spiritual, personal, and real presence of the Risen Lord in the world. What characterizes this presence and what distinguishes it from other forms, is that it is tied to the relationship of unity among the lives of human beings. This dynamic and collective aspect does not come as strongly into light in the eucharistic presence, or in the Word, or in the depths of each individual soul, and so on. On a number of occasions Chiara has used a comparison to illustrate this particular characteristic.

> Just as when [in the field of electricity] two poles are united, they produce light, two persons in grace, who unite in the name of Christ, experience a new life, a new strength. Christ was also present in them beforehand, in each one, as the energy within the two poles. However, the effect produced by unity is a greater one: Christ is in their midst.[1]

Let's begin then to examine what is required from two or more persons in order to have this presence of Christ among them; that is, in order to be united in the name of Jesus which Matthew 18:20 indicates. Afterward, we will examine the particular characteristics of this presence and the effects it produces.

The conditions

As we have seen above, what is required to live with Jesus in our midst is to be united in his name, which Chiara joins also to the new commandment of mutual love: "to the point of being consumed in unity." We have also seen that this is a vital reality that precedes the understanding itself of the verse of Matthew 18:20.[2]

In a writing of 1949, we find an explanation of what it means for people to be united in Jesus' name, so as to have him present among them.

> Jesus is among us when we are united in him, in his will, which means in his very self, and his will is that we love each other as he has loved us.
>
> The sentence of Jesus "Where two or more are gathered together in my name, there am I in the midst of them" goes side by side with another sentence, "Love one another *as* I have loved you."
>
> Therefore, the two of us, for example, are united in the name of Jesus if we love each other as he has loved us.
>
> Now, from this you will understand how even we who live in the focolare centers do not always have Jesus in our midst. To have him so, in every moment I would have to love you (presuming that it is just the two of us who live in a particular focolare center) as he loved us, and be loved in return by you *in the same way.*
>
> He loved us to the point of dying for us, and to the point of suffering above all else, the abandonment.[3]
>
> Not always, or rarely, does love for our neighbor require such sacrifice. However, if the love that I must have for you (that action which is an expression of love) does not *intentionally* contain the way of love with which he loved us, I do not love as he loves. If similarly, you do not love to this extent, then we are *not* united in his name and Jesus is not among us.[4]

23

To be united in Jesus' name, therefore, demands that we do his will, which is summed up in the new commandment of reciprocal love.

This is what Chiara unremittingly stresses in her book published in 1976, *Jesus in our Midst*.

> But what are the conditions for having Jesus in our midst? We know what they are: we have Jesus in our midst when we are united in his name. This means when we are united in him, in his will, in love which is his will, in reciprocal love which is the supreme will of Jesus, his commandment, where there is unity of sentiment, of will, of thought, possibly in all things, but decisively in matters of faith.[5]

Following this paragraph come various quotations of some of the Fathers of the Church, confirming one or the other of the conditions Chiara lists. She writes, "from this writing we note that one sees the same reality from a particular angle, and the other from another angle."[6]

"Reciprocal love," therefore, "where there is unity of sentiment, of will, of thought." Here lies the principal condition for the presence of Jesus in our midst which Chiara has underlined since the beginning, while explaining as years went by, its many nuances. Let's take a look at some of them.

First of all we see how, for Chiara, to love as Jesus loved us is not just a sentimental feeling, but implies the entire ascetical life of each person.

> And reciprocal love did not mean sentimentalism. It meant a constant sacrifice of one's entire self to live the life of the other. It meant the perfect renouncement of self. "If anyone wishes to be a follower of mine, let him renounce himself and take up his cross and follow me" (Mt 16:24); it meant to carry one another's burdens.[7]

An initial consequence of loving as Jesus did is the communion of spiritual and material goods.

> How did Jesus love us? What is the measure of his love for us? Death on the cross. We had to be ready to die for one another: "No one has greater love than this: to give one's life for one's friends."

Ready therefore for whatever small or great tribute of love for the other, since giving one's life was the measure.

Ready always to give material goods . . .

Ready to put our salaries in common, all the small and large goods that we had and would have acquired . . . Ready to put in common also our spiritual goods . . .[8]

. . . one's experiences for example; humbly offering the others what seemed an experience of life and the fruit of the *new self* in us.[9]

In describing the conditions for having the presence of Jesus in our midst Chiara speaks of "unity of sentiment, of will, of thought . . ." Unity, as we will see ahead, is fundamental for Chiara, and is viewed not only as a condition, but also as a fruit of the presence of Jesus in our midst. We will consider afterward the explanation which she herself gives to this fact and the supernatural nature of the unity of which she intends. For now we will present a few lines that describe in concrete terms this unity of sentiment, of will and of thought.

Already during the early years, we find the phrase "to be one with our neighbor" described in these terms:

To be one means to feel in ourselves the sentiments of the others. To resolve them as our own, made ours through charity. *To be them.* And this out of love for God, for Jesus in our neighbor.[10]

It is a "forgetting of ourselves":

To be one with our neighbor meant to forget ourselves completely. It meant to lose everything, even to put aside the things that were presently in our souls in order to live the sufferings and joys of the other, thus showing Jesus our love: to be crucified with him living in our neighbor, and to be joyful with him.[11]

This is what Chiara will have explained later on through the expression "to make ourselves one" in her book on charity.[12]

What we have described in these pages is the ascetics that each individual can and must live, but to have the presence of Jesus in our midst it is necessary that this kind of love become reciprocal.

To make ourselves one with our neighbors out of love for Jesus, with the love of Jesus, to the point that our neighbors . . . would want to make themselves one with us. . . . To the point of establishing these essential elements among the two so that the Lord might say of us: "Where two or more are gathered together in my name, there am I in the midst of them."[13]

In fact, to the specific question as to whether this disposition was sufficient if only found on one side, Chiara clearly responded: no, the other must be equally disposed to love in this way and that mutual love needs to be declared.[14]

This reciprocal "making ourselves one" demands that each be ready to lose one's own ideas and inspirations.[15] Unity of thought is reached by putting into common one's own ideas with this readiness to lose them.

Through this complete communion, which is the concrete actualization of reciprocal love, we will also arrive at being one soul, at having one thought, in which each individual thinks what the community thinks, and each one feels what the community feels. And it will be Christ who thinks in us, who plans and organizes in us the coming of his kingdom in the world.[16]

Chiara strongly insists on the importance of this aspect, referring back to the early Christians:

Reciprocal love brought everyone immediately . . . to one thought; not only, therefore, to one heart, but to one thought. And if we were not of one thought, this signified a disunity for us, which we needed to reconcile. . . .

To be one soul consists in having one way of thinking, of feeling, which is that of Jesus. If we are incorporated into Christ, if we are him, to have divisions and different thoughts means to divide Christ. And note that for St. Paul, this unity of thought did not regard only doctrinal matters, but all of life in its Christian practice.[17]

We note here that unity of thought is seen as a result of reciprocal love and at the same time an essential condition for being one soul.

There is another forcible expression that we find in Chiara which summarizes this unity of sentiment, will and thought, the conditions for having the presence of Jesus in our midst. What is necessary— she says—is the "total death of self, the emptying, out of love, of one's *entire* humanity in God."[18]

At first glance, such an expression might appear negative, and contrary to the modern mentality that wishes everyone to be fulfilled. This poverty of self, this "dying to self," more than being an ascetical effort, is seen by Chiara as a natural consequence of love, and therefore as something positive.

> What is necessary is the complete death to self. This does not mean, however, to stand there and kill ourselves—it serves no purpose—but rather in the sense of dying to self by living Christianity, which is love for others, the readiness to die for the others.[19]

On another occasion Chiara said, "In loving others, we burn ourselves away as a consequence."[20]

In conclusion, we can repeat with Chiara that the conditions required for having the presence of Jesus in our midst are not really that many, yet neither are they few. "They are all that we are and have because God wants our unity always aflame."[21]

How to reestablish the presence of Jesus in our midst when it is lacking

We have seen that the fundamental condition for having the presence of Jesus in our midst is reciprocal love to the point of being ready to give one's life for the others, which requires also the readiness to renounce our personality and ideas. Naturally, such a disposition cannot be reached once and forever. Jesus in our midst is a dynamic reality which necessitates a continuous effort of charity, and which implies also living the negative virtues in order to maintain it.

Just as two crossed logs feed a fire as they consume themselves, so too, if we want to live with Jesus constantly present in our midst, we must live moment to moment all the virtues (patience, prudence, meekness, poverty, purity, etc.) that are required for the soul so that the supernatural unity with one another is never diminished. Jesus in our midst cannot be established once and forever, because Jesus is life, he is dynamism.[22]

"A small lack in charity, a sentiment of pride, a possessive desire" is enough to impede the circulation of charity and therefore, the presence of Jesus in our midst.[23]

Jesus in our midst can vanish also due to a letdown of the common commitment "when, after an initial moment characterized by particular graces that God sends, there is no longer that complete casting of self into loving God with all one's heart, soul and strength and into loving our neighbor, and there is no longer that readiness to give one's life for the other, when—we can say—we give much, but not everything. And unity among us weakens, to the point of vanishing."[24]

In moments like these, how can we return to the fullness of Jesus in our midst? Chiara insists above all on the necessity of reestablishing unity before doing anything else whatsoever, using whatever means that is conforming to the gospel. "Like shipwrecked persons who cling to anything that will keep them afloat, we sought any means possible, suggested by the gospel, to rebuild our shattered unity."[25]

We will examine several of Chiara's explanations on how to go about it. First of all, it is always good to presuppose that the blame is also our own by "asking for pardon, taking the initiative, even when it is not we but our neighbor who may have had something against us. The gospel warns us that no offering at the altar is pleasing to God when made in an atmosphere that lacks reciprocal charity."[26]

If our neighbor had lacked charity, we were to be ready to fill in his or her part.

> We made a pact among ourselves: that the one who sees
> a fault in the other, a defect, would be the one who pays, the

one who fills in the missing part, naturally without becoming overbearing, but only *out of love*.[27]

Thus we help our neighbor return to a disposition of love.

If another is at fault, then let's double our charity in that person's regard. Without burdening the other to change, let's find a thousand ways suggested by love to help the other return to a disposition of love.[28]

If we realize that it is we who are at fault, we must ask forgiveness and reset ourselves in love.

If it is we who are at fault, we must immediately get back on our feet and choose God and love for our neighbor once again. We must recognize our mistaken conduct and set everything back in order, telling ourselves (one another) that we don't want Jesus to be absent from our midst for even a moment.[29]

This concrete methodology which Chiara suggests comes from years of experience, as does the following.

Some useful methods for maintaining and strengthening the presence of Jesus in our midst

To a group of youth who had asked her how to strengthen the presence of Jesus in their midst Chiara gave some profound suggestions which she drew from her experience. The first was to make a pact of mercy.

We made a kind of promise: to see each other as new everyday, as though we were meeting each other for the first time, unaware of the others' defects. We called it a pact of mercy.

Before going to bed at night, we buried all the impressions, faults and the judgments we noted regarding the persons with whom we lived. We awoke the next morning seeing the others new, as though they had never had any defects.[30]

Another method she suggested to the youth was the so-called moment of truth or reciprocal admonishment. In a former book, Chiara had explained how alive this aspect was among the early Christians and how it helped to maintain unity.

Another way of exercising reciprocal love, which was very present among the early Christians was reciprocal admonishment. . . .

I would like to emphasize how fraternal correction and mutual edification have always been essential elements for us since our very beginning.

It was the first thing we did whenever we met together; this kept unity among us alive.[31]

In essence, any kind of practice that brings Christ to live more in us has value in building unity, as does for example, living the word of God.

If we are the living word, that is, if we are not living our own selves, but we allow God's word to live in us, Christ is born in us.

Let's say that two young people meet each other along the street. Each one is living the word. Who lives in each of them? Christ. When they meet, because they are equal (both being Jesus), Jesus immediately loves Jesus. Therefore, when we live the word together, the presence of Jesus in our midst is automatic.[32]

Here Chiara makes a comparison, which first dates back to a writing of 1948:

We are united in the name of the Lord when we live the word of life which makes us *one*. . . .

I thought about how branches are engrafted, how the two cut parts of the branches, making contact with the two *living* parts become one.

When will two souls be consumed into one? When they are *living,* meaning when they are *cut* from what is merely human, and through living and incarnating the word of life, they become *living words*. Two *living words* can be consumed into one. If one is not *alive,* the other cannot unite itself to it.[33]

This life in the word of God is regarded as necessary for the presence of Jesus in our midst.

> To have Jesus in our midst, it is necessary that our spirits be always more attuned to the gospel, to everything that Jesus said. It is necessary that we be the living word of Jesus.[34]

Before concluding this section on the conditions required to have the presence of Jesus in our midst and on its dynamics, let's take a brief look at three other points.

Who is included in the words "Where two or three"?

The principal condition for having the presence of Jesus in our midst is to be "gathered together in his name" and we have spoken of various nuances of this. In this anonymous expression, Chiara sees that the possibility to live it is open to everyone.

> "Where two or three . . ." Jesus does not specify anyone in particular; the two or three are anonymous. "Where two or three . . ." whoever they are.
>
> Two or three repentant sinners who unite in his name; two or three young women, as we were during the war; two persons, one a grownup, the other a child. . . . Two or three . . .
>
> It was a spirituality which did not require any lengthy process of preparation, nor was it open exclusively to chosen souls or those already adept in spiritual matters. It seemed an ideal made for all. Jesus, in fact, did not say: "Where two or three *saints* are gathered in my name . . ." but "Where two or three . . ."[35]

Therefore, the possibility is open for universal application.

It is possible to have Jesus in our midst also over distance

In a letter attributed to the year 1957, Chiara had mentioned the possibility of having Jesus in our midst at a distance, saying: "Jesus can be among us, even though we are far from one another."[36] Later on, however, it no longer appeared to her that this was possible. Speaking of Jesus in our midst she said: "It is a particular presence that God gives to the community as such, that is, in the actual gathering together."[37]

A confirmation found in the writings of the Fathers of the Church led her back to this conviction in 1976:

> Athanasius applies Matthew 18:20 also to those who are far from one another, but spiritually united. This gives great joy to us. He says, "although distance divides us, nonetheless . . . the Lord . . . unites us spiritually in harmony and in the bond of peace. When we have these sentiments and raise the same prayers [to God], no distance can separate us, because the Lord unites us and binds us closely together. For where two or three are gathered in his name, he himself is present in the midst of them as he promised."[38]

Therefore, physical proximity is not required in order to have Jesus in our midst.

A presupposition: being in the state of grace

For Chiara, it is always understood that to have the presence of Jesus in our midst it is first of all necessary to be in the grace of God. In fact, she explains, Jesus in our midst is the life of grace set into motion, that is, the life of the mystical body.[39] Therefore, it is logical that this presupposes the life of grace in each individual.

Chiara had once specifically mentioned this condition also from a negative standpoint, saying, "perhaps we can never say *when* he is in our midst, because this presupposes the life of grace in us, and no one can be certain whether or not to be in the grace of God."[40]

Later, instead, we find this beautiful affirmation which implicitly contains this same truth, but in a positive light.

> The love that a Christian bears ... is a love of divine origin. It is God's own love shared with humankind on which it engrafts itself, thus making humankind a child of God.
>
> This is the premise and cause of an incomparable reality ... *supernatural brotherhood*.
>
> Now, in this brotherhood ... Christ blossoms within the midst of human lives, as the Emmanuel, God with us. In this brotherhood Christians are united in the name of Christ who said "Where two or three are gathered together in my name, there am I in the midst of them."[41]

To have this presence of Jesus in our midst, in fact, there must be reciprocal charity, but supernatural charity presupposes grace.

B. The Effects of the Presence of Jesus in Our Midst

"What are the effects that come from living the gospel sentence which says: 'Where two or three are gathered together in my name, there am I in the midst of them'?" asked someone recently to Chiara. Her answer sums up what we will present over the next set of pages.

> In putting into practice this word of the gospel, we have the presence of Jesus among us; not the presence of a particular virtue, but the presence of a person.
>
> With our own eyes we do not see his presence, but he is there and he examines our every thought, our every heartbeat, and he knows everything that regards our souls. He is there. He is in everyone, he embraces everyone, he assists, he enlightens, and he encourages each and everyone together ...
>
> And where he is found, there is the Church. ...
>
> And the Church, wherever found, irradiates his power. Christ acts as he acted when he was in Palestine, though under a different form.[42]

Therefore, we are speaking of a real and personal presence of Jesus which enlightens and encourages, an ecclesial presence that acts. Let us examine some other characteristics of this presence beginning with the effects that it produces.

As we mentioned above, Chiara and her first companions, in setting out to live the new commandment of Jesus, noticed that their lives took on a leap in quality without knowing the reason why. This was first experienced and only later linked with the presence of Jesus promised in Matthew 18:20. Chiara explains:

> We came to realize (in a very gentle way, because God acts gently, without force, bringing us only afterward to the awareness of what point he had led us to as we look over our shoulders and see what abyss we have left behind) what God had brought us to enjoy. As a new child naturally enjoys the light of life, we enjoyed his presence among us. . . .
>
> We didn't know what it was that gave such comfort to our souls, such light and security, such certainty about the new road we were taking. . . .
>
> We realized it only when it vanished . . . and the life we embarked on lost its meaning.[43]

In fact, it was this presence of his that gave meaning to everything, above all to this new choice of leaving everything for God.

> Only he gave meaning to our newly found brotherly and sisterly relationships. It surely would not have been worthwhile to leave our own fathers, mothers, brothers, sisters, our natural families, pleasing as they are to God, if it were not to belong to a supernatural family with Jesus in our midst.[44]

"But to know well what it is to have Jesus in our midst" Chiara affirms, "we have to experience it."[45] "Since he is not physically, but spiritually present, you cannot say he is this tall, and this handsome . . . or magnificent or that he speaks like such . . ."[46] To explain this experience, Chiara compares it to other spiritual phenomena, specifying that Jesus in our midst is sensed in a higher sphere of the soul.

> Just as a person feels joy, sorrow, anguish or doubt, so too—but in a higher part of the soul—we experienced the

peace that only the spiritual presence of Jesus in our midst could give; the fullness of joy to be found only in him, the vigor and conviction which are fruit not so much of reasoning or an effort of the will, but of a special help from God.[47]

She continues, describing other effects:

His presence was a more than sufficient recompense for any sacrifice that we made. It gave meaning and purpose to every step along the way that we took toward him for his sake. It enabled us to see things and circumstances in their proper perspective, comforted us in our troubles, and tempered any excessive rejoicing.[48]

We will now consider one by one some of these principal effects.

Jesus in our midst enlightens

First of all, this experience showed that Jesus in our midst is *light for understanding the Scriptures and the teachings of the Church.* Already back in 1950, Chiara describes "the light of his that made us see his words as being so beautiful, revolutionary, necessary and vital to our becoming true Christians."[49]

Later on she wrote:

Just as in the beginning it seemed that our deepened understanding of the Scriptures must have been due to the presence of Jesus among us, so too, we felt it must have been this same presence that enabled us to understand more profoundly the words of the Holy Father and the bishops.[50]

Chiara cites a confirmation of this in the Fathers of the Church.

Origen says that Jesus, present among those united in his name, is ready "to illumine the hearts of those who truly desire to understand his teaching." With these words he leads us to understand that he is not speaking of just an intellectual enlightenment, but of a vital and sapiential illumination that extends to the whole person.[51]

Chiara describes this as a "kind of exegesis" that Jesus makes.

And this presence of his influenced the understanding of his word. He was the Teacher who showed us how to understand his words. In other words, this was a type of exegesis made not by a theology professor, but rather by Christ himself.[52]

Furthermore, the light of Jesus in our midst enlightens our minds and provides wisdom for us and for others. In 1950 Chiara wrote:

United in the charity of Christ, who gives us God's presence, we give all of ourselves so that the light of Jesus might enlighten the minds of many.[53]

And she speaks of wisdom, "which is born, reigns, and triumphs only where there is Jesus in the midst,"[54] font of wisdom, which, provided we do not lose his presence, "will flow continuously in our minds and overflow onto others."[55]

Here Chiara describes how this wisdom gives order to all things:

When Jesus is among us, *wisdom*, with ceaseless activity, seems to order all things. Each one shares in it, rejoices because of it and feels, wherever he or she may be, to be occupying the right place, the place God wants.[56]

Jesus in our midst also enlightens our consciences. His presence "is like the loudspeaker of Jesus in each soul" which "makes his voice within us grow and makes us better able to receive it: to receive and consequently to live the new self in us."[57]

It is a light that guides us:

And when the course of action to take is unclear, to whom else do we turn but to him, saying amongst ourselves: "Come, let's put Jesus in our midst so we can understand the will of God."

He alone is the light of our life, the solution to our every problem.

Origen, too, realized this when he wrote: "If there is an uncertainty which we are unable to resolve or find an explanation for, let us go, united in heart in regards to the question at hand to Jesus, who is present where two or three are gathered together in his name, and is ready by his presence in power to illumine hearts . . . that they might deeply penetrate the matter."[58]

Not only does he guide us for what regards our own life, but also on how to bring others to God. Therefore he is our leader, who infuses a divine strategy in us.

If you want to win a city over to Christ's love . . . take some friends that have the same feelings as you. Join together with them in Christ's name. . . . Promise one another perpetual, constant love so that the world's conqueror will always be among you as your leader.[59]

Speaking about this "invisible leader," Chiara elsewhere also says: "He will suggest to us what we must do, what other steps to take, as a divine strategist who holds a universal view."[60]

Jesus in our midst brings joy

Another effect of Jesus in our midst is joy.

Jesus is always life and fullness, joy and paradise, guide and master. Our reciprocal love can be the powerful means to render him present.[61]

In fact we mentioned above about a "fullness of joy" that can only be found in God.[62]

Later on Chiara explains this phenomenon with the help of one of the Fathers of the Church. Jesus in our midst is Jesus of the resurrection.

When Jesus is in our midst, there is always a festive atmosphere.

If there is one thing characteristic of our meetings, both small and large, it is the fullness of joy that emanates from each person, that lights up each face. . . .

Yes, because Jesus in the midst of a small group or a large number gathered together in his name is Jesus of the resurrection, who now, besides living at the right hand of the Father, also lives in the little churches made up of several Christians.

St. John Chrysostom says: "Even though Pentecost day is over, the feast is not at an end; whenever we assemble there is festivity. From what do we deduce this? From the very words of Christ who says, 'where two or three are gathered together in my name, there am I in the midst of them.' Therefore, each time that Christ is present in the midst of a gathering, what greater proof could you ask than that there be a festive atmosphere?"[63]

Jesus in our midst is a source of strength and consolation

We spoke before about a strength that exceeds human strength, and which comes as a special help from God.[64] Let's look at a more detailed description.

Jesus in the midst gave strength to whoever was called to leave one's family: "every detachment became easy because Jesus was in the midst of persons united in his name."[65]

Besides shedding light on the gospel, "he gave us the strength, through the gift of the Holy Spirit, to put into practice what we read."[66]

He was a support in moments of struggle and trial.

Nothing seemed to better sustain us in the struggles and trials of trying to promote goodness amidst a corrupt and atheistic society than this new strength that Jesus offered to our fraternal collectivity.[67]

Finally, he is said to be a consoler.

For us, Jesus in our midst was a great consoler, and therefore will always be so for you too.[68]

Jesus in our midst brings peace

We have seen how already in 1948 Chiara spoke of unity and of Jesus in our midst, saying, "He is peace, joy, love, ardor."[69] We also listed as one of the principal fruits of Jesus in our midst, "that peace which is his alone."[70] But let's take a look at a more in-depth explanation. Chiara was asked, "How can we know whether his presence is there or not?" In her answer she describes peace as something that Jesus in our midst gives in a very particular way.

> Peace for the soul is like health for the body: peace is the health of the soul. Normally, we don't *feel* healthy, but we do *feel* sick; so too, in the same way we don't *feel* peace, but we do *feel* the lack of it. Therefore, when you are gathered together, whether at home, or on the streets, or at work, and you assess that there is peace, rest assured. If there is peace Jesus is present, because he is peace.
>
> You don't have to experience great sensations. The supernatural is not always something to be felt.[71]

Peace seen as the fullness of Christian life is the way Chiara spoke of it years prior during an informal talk.

> It seems to me that we should not attach ourselves to the effects of Jesus in our midst, but rather to Jesus in our midst. . . . How peaceful Jesus appears to be . . . think of the thirty years he lived in Nazareth where no one realized who he was. It was a miracle that he was hidden in that manner; but he was not hiding, he lived amidst all the others. Therefore, he lived in a state of normality. He was God. You will understand that if he who was even physically present lived in a state of normality, he will also in his spiritual presence bring our souls to a state of normality. We who come from the state of original sin are the ones unfamiliar with the state of normality, because coming from the world, we believe that the world is an expression of normality. No, the world is in a state of abnormality, while the state of Christian being is the true normality.[72]

Jesus in our midst is therefore the normality of Christian life lived in its fullness. Peace is its effect.

As at Emmaus

The effects considered until now, of light, joy, and strength, are summed up well in a comparison Chiara made during her trip to the Holy Land in 1960. As Chiara walked along the road the two disciples had taken on their way to Emmaus, she connected that event with the presence of Jesus in our midst whose effects are similar to those brought about by the appearance of the Risen Lord described in Luke 24:13–35. Chiara drew attention to the episode where Jesus explains the Scriptures, and where the two disciples implore him, "Stay with us," followed by their final comment "weren't our hearts burning inside us as he talked to us on the road." Chiara states:

> There are probably no better words than these to explain the experience that we have had from the time we started living with Jesus in our midst. Jesus is always himself, and even when he is present only spiritually, he explains the Scriptures to us, and our hearts burn with the charity of Christ, which is the true life. Once we have known him in this way, we are tempted to say, with infinite nostalgia: "Stay with us, for it is growing toward evening, and without you, there surely will come the dark of night."[73]

Jesus in our midst paves the way to sanctity

Since the early years, Jesus in our midst has been seen as a means of sanctification: "*Jesus among us* as the premise or principle , as the means of sanctification and as the end."[74]

Later, during an informal conference, Chiara explained the dynamics of this spiritual growth.

Similarly, as when you go out into the sun you do not remain unchanged, for your skin gets darker, if you live in a focolare center where you do everything possible to allow Jesus to be present among you, your souls undergo—as St. Teresa says—a dilation. They continually expand, so that one day your capacity to suffer for the Church will be greater, because your capacity to love is greater. If there is Jesus in our midst in our focolare center, the life of grace in us does not remain static. Since the presence of Jesus in our midst necessitates a continuous choice on our own part, we must be continually dead in order to be alive, and thus we continually grow.[75]

Besides our own effort at work, however, there is also the very same presence of Jesus that operates, too. "It is possible to become saints if Jesus is always in our midst" Chiara writes, "because it will be he, the Saint, who will infect us with his sanctity."[76] "He will be the one to teach us to be perfect"[77] and "it is he who makes the world around us disappear and opens up the beauty of the interior world."[78]

Finally, we should emphasize how Jesus in our midst leads the way to a sanctity that is not only individual, but collective.

We began to understand, in fact, that even our own personal sanctification would be achieved by loving others as ourselves. This is what would insure our progress through the various stages of the spiritual life. . . .

It became increasingly evident that God was urging us to search for his kingdom not only within ourselves, but also in our midst. We would make the kingdom grow inside us by trying to establish it among ourselves. The journey toward God was not to be made alone, but together. We were not to seek to become saints on our own, but in company with others, with many others.[79]

Through this full communion of soul, which is the result of reciprocal love, says Chiara, "we will learn that great and newest form of art, still unknown to the world: that of becoming saints together. Christ, the Saint, will be in our midst; he will live in each one of us."[80]

Jesus in our midst brings about conversions

Besides the effects we experience in and among us when we live with Jesus in our midst, there are also many fruits that blossom around us, above all in the form of conversions.

In a letter already in 1948, Chiara pictured Jesus in our midst as a whirlpool that draws the objects around it into its swirl. She comments: "So too, each soul who meets Jesus (Jesus among us) will be irretrievably lost in his love."[81]

In that same period she speaks of a fire that he brings.

> If we are united—and we do not break this unity for any reason whatsoever, whether within or around us—Jesus will be in our midst and he will set everything aflame. He came only to bring fire upon the earth and nothing else does he desire than that it be already set aflame. . . .
>
> Let's be confident. He will overcome the world and will do greater things than those he once performed. He said so himself.[82]

This conviction certainly goes back to the experience of those early years. In fact, Chiara speaks of "seven, fifteen, one hundred, five hundred, one thousand, three thousand and more people of every vocation and every social condition," which "grew day by day around Jesus among us"[83] and comments: "We soon realized that this was the true apostolate."[84]

Chiara describes how the light of Jesus in our midst would bring about true conversions:

> From this cell of the mystical body that we comprised, there emanated a light which good and simple people around us who were searching for God, like sinners for example who were humbled by the weight of their sins, had recognized as the light of Jesus. This light was so striking to those coming from secular backgrounds that it was often a contributing factor to conversions. People who were before attached to thousands of things experienced a new reality, one which, even if unaware, they always longed for. This reality, which is Jesus, is the only one which could satisfy them.

That light changed everything, revolutionized everything.[85]

Jesus, truly present, bears testimony to himself.

It is Jesus who touches hearts, and he alone knows how to convert people, he alone can truly bear witness to himself. . . .

Few remain indifferent when they come in contact with Jesus present in a small or large community. Jesus, who is Light, manifests himself. He who is Fire, gives warmth. Many who never really believed in him, begin to believe, because now in a certain way, spiritually speaking, he can be seen.[86]

Therefore, the presence of Christ in our unity is the explanation for the many conversions. The witness of unity is very suitable to our times. In fact, Chiara was asked, "What do you believe is the most effective and suitable means to make Christ known to the world today?" Her response: "A people that is united in the name of the Father, the Son, and the Holy Spirit," and she goes on to describe the Church which is alive where two or three are united in the name of Christ, and which is alive "through the reciprocal love among its members . . . through the unity it creates."[87] In a talk given in 1961, almost foreshadowing *Gaudium et Spes,* section 21e, Chiara said:

The greatest witness to the existence of God that we can give the world—since God is pure spirit—is that of living in such a way as to have his presence in our midst. In this way, he bears witness to himself. Just as today a kind of collective spirituality has developed around atheism, God also wanted to be testified through a community that carried his presence in its midst. It is a return to the spirit of the early Christians, who themselves bore witness to unity.[88]

This is the explanation to John 17:21: "May they may be one in us, that the world may believe that you sent me." "The world around us, witnessing unity," Chiara writes, "came to join us."[89] This is also confirmed as the characteristic apostolate of the Focolare in its rule:

The union of souls in the name of Christ is what characterizes the entire apostolate of the Work of Mary, and in such union lies the roots of the apostolate's vitality, as we find it expressed in Jesus' words: "This is how all will know you for my disciples: by your love for one another" (Jn 13:35), and "that they may be one in us, that the world may believe that you sent me" (Jn 17:21).[90]

Here it is important to note that the conversions that are a fruit of Jesus in our midst far outweigh the sum of all the individual efforts involved, proof that they are a work of God.

There are focolare centers whose members live in unity, and though lacking in maturity and coming from sinful pasts of little meaning, they have Jesus in their midst. They have Life.

On the other hand, there can be beautiful souls, great and saintly souls, but if they do not live in unity, they do not bring about the conversions or other fruits typical of unity. Conversions are truly a work of God who is present where there is unity.[91]

Addressing herself to the members of the Focolare, Chiara spoke of "the miracles of conversions to God, and the previously unimagined transformations due to the word that you announced united with Jesus in your midst."[92]

Finally, we note that the conversions that occurred because of this presence are many and varied. Chiara speaks of the "conversions of sinners, of atheists; the lukewarm who become ardent, those who thought themselves to be good become apostles of the love of Christ and neighbor,"[93] and she says they are "countless."[94]

Jesus in our midst obtains graces

Since the very beginning, the words of Matthew 18:20 had explained and enlightened for Chiara the words of the previous verse: "Again I tell you, if two of you join your voices on earth to pray for anything whatsoever, it shall be granted you by my Father in heaven" (Mt 18:19).

There is a prayer which members of the Focolare have been using for thirty years now, since its very beginning. If you ask them to pray in any kind of circumstance, for the living or for the dead, or to obtain any grace at all, they make—as we know—a *consenserint*; that is, united in the name of Jesus, they ask the eternal Father for anything whatsoever.[95]

Chiara explains:

In this prayer we know that we are not the ones who ask, but Jesus present in our unity.[96]

And she finds that the Fathers of the Church confirm this.

John Chrysostom says that no one meets together with others to pray "trusting in one's own virtue," but rather in the community, in agreement, which God holds in the highest consideration and by which he is moved and appeased.

"'For where two or three are gathered together in my name'—he [Jesus] said—'there am I in the midst of them . . .' What, in fact, cannot be obtained by praying alone, will be obtained by praying together with many. Why? Because although there is not great strength in personal virtue, there is in unanimity— 'where two or three are gathered together . . .' "[97]

Chiara also evidences the "truly evangelical breadth" of the words "anything whatsoever."

"Anything," therefore, everything. From little things to big ones; from things for our bodies to things for our spirits. Everything can be asked for in unity. And everything has been asked for in unity.[98]

Here she underlines, however, the necessity to live the gospel in its entirety:

Of course, we always thought that the above-mentioned statement of the gospel obtains its end if you live it along with all the rest of the gospel. For this reason, before making a *consenserint*, we examine ourselves to see if we are ready to die for one another, and we do not slacken this readiness after having prayed.[99]

Jesus in our midst brings about unity

We have seen that for Chiara, unity is the condition for having the presence of Jesus in our midst, but unity is also one of the effects of this presence. She affirms, for example, that he brings "to our actions unity of heart, of will, and unity of mind"[100] and that it was he "who formed unity among us—the unity that he brought into this world."[101] In the next chapter we will take a closer look at the nature of this unity, which reflects the life of the Trinity. For now let us turn to the fulfillment of Jesus' prayer (Jn 17:21) and how Chiara sees it as being a consequence of Jesus in our midst.

First of all, she attributes the very understanding of this passage to the presence of Jesus in their midst.

It was his presence among us that helped us understand the significance of the words in his priestly prayer: "That they may all be one."[102]

Here is a text which tells what followed as a result of this understanding:

I recall how we understood that the unity Jesus asked of us was something truly celestial, so much so that one day as the Focolarine gathered in church together, they turned to God united in Jesus' name and asked him: "Fulfill your testament in us, as you see it, for we do not know what it means; we know that it is something very lofty, and divine, but fulfill it as you know it to be. And through us, extend it to all the earth."[103]

For Chiara, it is precisely Jesus in our midst, who fulfills this prayer. She writes, "It seems to us, in fact, that only with Jesus in our midst can the unity invoked by Christ before his death be fully realized."[104] In fact, experiencing unity among several people, she understood that it is possible among a greater number, among everyone, and thus comes to affirm: "Our living with Jesus in our midst . . . gave us the certainty that one day, perhaps afar, unity will be accomplished."[105]

Having seen what is required in order to have the presence of Jesus in our midst, and the effects that it produces, let's attempt to define, in Chiara's words, the nature of this presence.

A personal and real presence

Above all we should take note of the ontological reality of this presence of Christ for Chiara; it is both personal and real. "Jesus in our midst is not just a norm or a rule," she writes, "though it's true that he does precede every other rule. Jesus in our midst is a person! The most holy person of Jesus."[106]

The following verses, included in a Christmas greeting of 1974, can tell us how real for Chiara is the presence of Jesus in the midst of two or more. It is the same Jesus that was among Mary and Joseph at Bethlehem.

"Where two or three are gathered together
in my name, there am I
in the midst of them."
In the midst of them just as he was
in the midst of Mary and Joseph
two thousand years ago.
The only difference is that his presence now,
though real, is spiritual.
Jesus does not want to remain

only within the tabernacle.
He desires to be present among human beings.
To share their thoughts, their plans,
their concerns, their joys . . .
He came to earth also for this:
to provide us with the possibility of having him
always in our midst, to bring the warmth,
hope, light and harmony
that comes with every Christmas.[107]

With this awareness of the reality of his presence among united Christians and imagining what sentiments might have been his in leaving his apostles behind, Chiara writes:

> We might say that before dying Jesus could have said, "Love God." But instead, he said, "Love one another." He was a man. He was their teacher, their father, their everything for whom they left all things. He loved them and suffered at seeing them orphans and suggested the best means by which they might continue to have God with them, since, "Where there is charity and love, there is God" and "Where two or more are gathered together in my name, there am I in the midst of them."[108]

To give us an idea as to the extent of which the presence of Jesus in our midst for Chiara is an ontological reality, let's take note of the value she places on it.

> If we are united, Jesus is among us. This is important. It is worth more than any other treasure that our hearts may possess—more than our mother, father, brothers, sisters, children. It is worth more than our house, our work, or our property; more than the artistic works in a city like Rome; more than our business deals; more than nature that surrounds us with flowers and fields; the sea and the stars; more than our own soul![109]

It is a reality of our faith, based on Jesus' words.

> He said it himself. And we believe him. It depends on our hearts, or better, on Christian reciprocal love which, if con-

taining the elements required by Jesus, bears as a consequence the most sweet and marvelous reality of our faith: "there am I in the midst of them."[110]

But it is also an existential experience. In the preceding section, we listed all its perceivable effects. The seriousness of Chiara's faith in the reality of this presence and the depth of her experience of it come across in her statement on death:

I too desire to have someone beside my deathbed (if I die in bed), who will help me to keep Jesus constantly in our midst. Then, indeed, death will only be a transition and the words "life merely changes" will become a personal experience.[111]

Jesus in our midst is one form of presence of the Risen Lord

Chiara writes:

Without our doing a lot of theological or philosophical reasoning, throughout the history of the Focolare we always understood that the presence of Jesus wasn't limited to a mere physical presence, formerly in history and now in heaven. There was the presence of Jesus in the midst of two or more persons, Jesus in the eucharist, Jesus in his word, Jesus in our neighbor, Jesus in the hierarchy.[112]

There has always been this presence, but it has now come more in evidence.

In the Church, the reality of Jesus in our midst has always existed, along with the truth of Jesus in our midst and the life of Jesus in our midst.... However, it was not given the emphasis that it is given today.... Jesus has always been in the midst of his Church, otherwise the Church would have fallen apart. It's just that now we realize more fully what this truth is, and therefore, we put it more into practice. Similarly, the twelfth century came to appreciate more fully the reality of the eucharist. Its value became more evident through the lives of mystics and then the work of theologians. As a result, appreciation of the eucharist increased, but it had always been there before.[113]

The various forms of Jesus' presence, for Chiara, can be seen in function of this particular one. In fact, she says:

It appears to me that we can show how all the presences of Jesus are in function of Jesus in our midst, because in the next life there will no longer be the hierarchy, nor the sacraments. There will be God—in the midst of his people.[114]

It is a dynamic presence

We have seen above that having the presence of Jesus in our midst requires a continuous effort. It is a presence which can also become weakened; therefore, it is life with its own dynamism.[115] This intrinsic dynamism expresses itself also in a dynamic projection outward, as this meditation says:

However, this fraternal communion is not a static happiness. It is a perennial quest not only resulting in the continuity of communion, but in spreading it to many others, because this communion is love. It is charity. And charity is diffusive by its very nature.[116]

His presence is a grace

In a talk given in 1961, Chiara poses this question: Is the presence of Jesus in our midst a grace? Or does Jesus come simply when we want to be one? Her answer: "It is a grace. This grace is Jesus who manifests himself. . . . Jesus in our midst is a grace; we must create the conditions so that this grace may come."[117]

Some time later, Chiara quotes Congar who gives a theological explanation that speaks of a "covenant structure."

> In this, we find a covenant structure (people meet together in the name of Jesus—Jesus becomes present in their midst) comparable, on its own level, to that of more institutional, i.e., juridical form, the covenant structure constituted by the sacraments or by the hierarchical ministries.

> "This is exactly what the Fathers understood. . . . According to them, where these conditions have been fulfilled and these covenant structures respected, i.e., brotherly love and the fraternal gathering of two or three in his name, the Lord carries out his promise, which in effect is bound to these conditions," that is, he becomes present.[118]

What is the meaning of "in our midst"?

Jesus in our midst is an expression which until now is little used in theology. We could ask ourselves what do these words mean for Chiara.

Back in 1948, she had already written:

> When two persons meet in the name of Christ, Christ is born among them; that is, *in them*. In maintaining this unity, they can sincerely say: "It is no longer I who live but Christ who lives in me."[119]

Soon afterward, she gave this clarification:

> Among you—who are united in his name—there is Jesus: you form Jesus, and Jesus cannot but live the life of Jesus![120]

Therefore, it is "being Christ" singularly and all together.

This following writing from 1950 speaks of Jesus in our midst as Jesus in us who brings us to live in him and who makes us one.

> Jesus in our midst meant Jesus in us ("may they all be one, Father, may they be one in us, as you are in me and I am in you . . . that they may be one as we are one"), made one by

him through mutual love and made sharers of his light, strength, love and, "I have given them the glory that you gave to me," therefore one among us.[121]

The expression "Jesus in our midst" comprises the aspects of "Christ in us" and "we in Christ." In fact, Chiara speaks of "Christ in our midst, in whom we too are engrafted,"[122] and also "He is in us; we are enveloped by him; we are inside of him."[123]

Therefore, it is not a physical "in our midst."

> It isn't that Jesus finds an empty space to occupy in our midst; it is not a physical "in our midst" . . . The words "in our midst" intend to say that he is in us; Jesus is in the midst of us. We all together share of him, as does each one of us; we partake of his presence. So it's not that Jesus finds an emptiness. I think he finds rather a fullness of love, and that it is this fullness of love that attracts him.[124]

In the above passage, we again find joined in the life of Christ the participation of the individual and that of the community.

Finally, we cite this unique explanation that Chiara gives of Jesus in our midst, from another point of view.

> It is God who makes two one, and who places himself as a third, as the relation between them: Jesus among them.[125]

A presence that presupposes the collectivity: the life of the mystical body in action

This is perhaps the characteristic element that distinguishes the presence of Jesus in our midst from other forms of his presence. "It is a presence of Jesus that presupposes the collectivity, at least of two persons," explained Chiara. "It is the particular grace of the presence of Jesus that already lies within the mystical body, but that comes to surface when two or more are united in his name."[126]

This concept is spelled out very well in a meditation of hers, where she adopts the use of a metaphor:

The communion of saints, the mystical body, does exist, but it is like a network of unlighted tunnels. The power that could light them up exists. The life of grace is present in many. But Jesus wanted more than this when he prayed to the Father. He wanted heaven on earth, the unity of all people with God and with one another: the tunnels lit up; the presence of Jesus in every relationship as well as in every soul.[127]

With the first set of approvals of the statutes of the Focolare, the Church gave a certain confirmation to this specific characteristic of Jesus in our midst. Article 9, after citing Matthew 18:20, speaks of the "mutual and continuous charity which, in the meaning intended by Jesus and taught by the Church, renders possible the presence of Jesus in the collectivity."[128] Commenting on this, Chiara notes that it is the first time that "Jesus in the midst of the collectivity" is spoken of, and that because of the approval of this rule on the part of the concilar congregation, it acquires a certain authority.[129]

Finally, let's recall, as we have seen above, the description of Jesus in our midst as "the health of the mystical body."[130] It is, says Chiara, "living as a mystical body by everyone, from whatever social condition or vocation."[131]

Other comparisons

To describe the presence of Jesus in our midst Chiara often uses metaphors and comparisons. Let's take a look at a few more of them in order to help us get a better picture of what the presence of Jesus in our midst is.

a) Like a fire

Chiara often compares Jesus in our midst to fire. Already in the early years, she spoke of charity as being a flame that unites.

Oh! then, how great will be the flame of divine charity in us. How much Jesus will grow in you and will devour you all.

Let him grow, and let yourselves die. Allow the charity that he has poured into your hearts to become aflame and spread, that it might spark from your eyes, your words, and your actions ... the charity that unites hearts and which draws everyone to having one thought alone: his, a single desire: his![132]

When we are united, this fire is Jesus himself among us.

United, they formed a hearth of charity whose fire was Jesus among them.[133]

It is a fire that fuses us.

Before we were mixed amongst one another like brothers and sisters; afterward Jesus in our midst was like a fire that melts two metals into a third, with different qualities than its original two components.[134]

We already cited a passage that speaks of crossed logs, burned by the fire of Jesus in our midst.[135] Let's look at another beautiful metaphor which speaks of a fire on the mountain top.

If you cross a few logs together on a mountain top, and then set fire to them, the flames will be seen throughout the length and the breadth of the valley, shining as brightly as a star fallen to earth. But,if we cross our hearts in a similar way, and love each other as he has loved us, we shall have *the* fire, love itself, among us, and we shall be instruments of God for many souls.[136]

We have spoken before of Jesus in our midst who ignites the world around us.[137] This additional passage emphasizes the fact that the fire of this conflagration is irresistible, because it is Jesus himself.

No one can put out its fire if it is a true fire. This fire has been set by Jesus, by Jesus in the midst of people wherever they may be; and that means an authentic fire.[138]

b) We form a living temple

This image, much used by St. Paul, is taken up by Chiara in reference to Jesus in our midst.

I implore you, keep *Jesus among you* by remaining always, all of you, *united in his name. . . .*

Remain in his love—by loving one another as he loved each of you—and then his and our Ideal will triumph and your whole college will become a focolare center—a living temple of the Holy Spirit of which you will be its living stones.[139]

Speaking also of the focolare center, Chiara underlines that it is not built with stones, but "we are the living stones, the temple of God, we who must hold Jesus tightly in our midst."[140]

This spiritual temple can be built anywhere.

Jesus among Christians was like a temple resting on firm pillars—the hearts of his children united together—that could be set up in any locality and provide the consolation of a spiritual tabernacle, whether out in the noisy streets, in secular societies or in the prison cells of those suffering unjustly for their convictions.[141]

c) It brings us to live in the Father's house

We are homeless and even here on earth we could all be in the Father's warm house, in anticipation of heaven, if we lived in that mystical but true reality of being relatives of Christ and of one another, and if we rediscovered ourselves as brothers and sisters, and brought the family together again with the presence of Christ among us along with the circulation of material and spiritual goods among us all.[142]

Here Chiara recalls, however, that Jesus in our midst is not a permanent home, but "comforting company."

I don't have a home. My home is in heaven. There is no sense deceiving ourselves that we have a home here below, where everything passes and where our family is not all together and Mary herself is missing, our mother who is living now in our heavenly home.

As daily food for our "journey" we have the eucharist; for a road to follow we have his divine will; for comforting company, Christ in the midst of the souls that God puts beside me.[143]

d) The kingdom of God

Through God's presence among us, we bring his kingdom into the world.

> We truly bring the kingdom of God on earth. In fact, God is among us, and through us this current of love (which is the current of trinitarian love) passes through the world in all the members of the mystical body, enlightening all things.[144]

Chiara speaks of "two fires: Jesus within us, Jesus among us" as "two aspects of the kingdom of God in us and among us."[145] She affirms:

> Anyone of us who, without overrationalizing or complicating things, believes in his words with the simple fascination of a child and puts them into practice could enjoy this foretaste of paradise: the kingdom of God in the midst of those who are united in his name.[146]

Finally, we note the concrete explanation that Chiara gives to this reality: "the kingdom of God" is "where God reigns." Where everything else is secondary to his presence in our midst.[147]

e) As in heaven

We have spoken above about this experience of the kingdom as "a foretaste of heaven." Here are a few other descriptions connected with the kingdom.

> Jesus in our midst! It is heaven on earth. It's well worth it to work hard at keeping mutual charity so as to experience a bit of heaven already here on earth.[148]
>
> When Jesus is present among two or more united in this way, he is the heaven that envelopes them, the heaven among them. It is Jesus who spiritually becomes present among them, a bit like at Emmaus. He ignites hearts with a flame that the world does not know, taking away our own manner of seeing people and things while bringing into relief only what is great, good and beautiful in the eyes of God.[149]

f) An experience of philadelphia

From another point of view, Jesus in our midst is described as a strong experience of *philadelphia* (brotherly love).

> He [Jesus in our midst], I realize, bonds me to others in a way that is both human and divine together. It is really an experience of philadelphia. So much so—as has happened to me in London—when it is time to depart, it's up to me to make the step "to lose," because of the great nostalgia I feel in wanting to stay behind with them. It is proof again for me that heaven exists, where this will be our experience, and that it is eternal. Here we are only on a journey.[150]

In this present section, we have listed various elements that describe the presence of Jesus in our midst and the effects it produces. To draw a conclusion and to introduce the next chapter, which considers "the profound reality of Jesus in our midst," we cite this one last paragraph, written in 1951. Chiara's definition of a focolare center in some way sums up what has been said thus far.

> The focolare center is a little heaven where Jesus in the midst of its members united in his name is *perennial light*, and the *perfect joy* promised to those who are consumed into one. He is *fruitfulness* in the apostolate because Jesus who lives in everyone cannot but overcome the world. He is *abundance* because where his kingdom is sought, the rest will also come; he is the *hope* of resurrection because anyone who lives with him, rises with him. He is the *certainty* of a heavenly inheritance, because the one who rises with him, is coheir with him. The focolare center becomes the kingdom of God. . . . Amongst it members lives . . . the first born brother, Jesus in their midst.[151]

Chapter 2

THE PROFOUND REALITY OF
JESUS IN OUR MIDST

We have thus far considered the life of Jesus in our midst from the standpoint of its conditions (how to have this presence) and its effects. We tried to grasp, through Chiara's writings and thoughts, its ontological reality.

In this chapter we would like to take a further step in understanding what this presence is and the life of communion that is linked to it.

Before going ahead, let's first call to mind a point that was mentioned in the general introduction concerning the years 1949–51. It was a period for Chiara marked by particular graces of light that strongly underlined the life she had already set out upon and which also gave a sketch of God's plan for the Focolare, then only in its early stages. Our focus will not be centered on the historical context of what occurred, but on several writings of that period which relate to our present theme.

At the outset, it is interesting to note that Chiara attributes this period of contemplation to Jesus in their midst. She describes it saying, "It was a beam of light. That is why there was such contemplation. . . . It was not just a thread of light. We were united. It was Christ in our midst."[1]

Elsewhere she explains that this "heaven" which God opened up for them ("through a special grace, because the Focolare needed this grace") was not one that was present in an individual soul. "It was one which was present in the midst of souls, it was truly Jesus in our midst who unveiled himself and in some way let himself be seen."[2]

Describing further what had happened, she adds, "The Spirit of God, which was stronger than all our own spirits, fused us into one and I called this 'the Soul,' with a capital S. This Soul—was us! . . . Jesus in our midst."[3]

The reality, therefore, already being lived with Jesus in their midst, became even clearer. "We had the impression," Chiara writes, "that the Lord opened the eyes of our souls to the kingdom of God which was among us: the Trinity indwelling in a cell of the mystical body.... 'Father, that they may be one even as we are one.' "[4]

Let's now consider three different themes that will help us grasp the reality of Jesus in our midst in this profound dimension: "The life of unity and trinitarian life," "Jesus in our midst and the Holy Spirit," and "Jesus in our midst and Jesus forsaken."

A. LIFE OF UNITY AND TRINITARIAN LIFE

One of Chiara's fundamental intuitions is precisely that of the primary importance of unity. On one occasion she describes, in fact, how she understood that God's "primary mode of seeing" is unity, so therefore, "if two minds unite through Christ in their midst, it may seem that in doing so they mortify themselves, but instead they are empowered, because they become closer to the mind of God."[5]

Already in a writing entitled "Unity" dated 1946, passages of which were referred to in the introduction,[6] we see how fundamental for Chiara this underlying concept of unity is. For a more complete view, we will cite a few other passages of that same writing.

> Unity can be found only where personality no longer exists.
>
> It is not a mixture that we must compose, but a combination, and this will occur only when each component, by the heat of the flame of divine love, loses itself for unity.
>
> What remains when two or more souls are combined? Jesus—Oneness....
>
> A person who is fused in unity loses everything, but every loss is a gain.
>
> Unity requires souls who are ready to lose their own personalities, entirely.
>
> It is because unity is God, and God is *one and triune.*
>
> Because of their very same nature, which is love, the three live unifying themselves (by emptying themselves) and in

doing so they each re-find themselves: $3 \rightarrow 1 \rightarrow 3$. The three make themselves one out of love, and in the One Love, they rediscover themselves.[7]

A few days later Chiara adds:

> Only Christ makes one entity from two. It is because Christ makes persons "dead to themselves" and "alive to grace," which is love.
>
> For us, to be of Christ, we must be *one* with our neighbors. Not in an ideal way, but in a real way. Not in the future, *but in the present. . . .*
>
> It means we must undo our hearts of stone, and acquire *hearts of flesh* that can love our neighbors.
>
> "Let's love with deeds and with the truth." Not, " Let's perform deeds and speak the truth." Instead, *we must love.* What counts is *to love.* And our deeds must have as their end, not the deed itself, but Jesus in our neighbor—the neighbor with whom we will be one out of love for Jesus.[8]

Chiara concludes by linking unity with Jesus' final prayer.

> All great persons, wherever they go, transform their environment and leave behind a mark of their race.
>
> Jesus was of heavenly origins, and having come to earth, does everything possible to bring to this new environment what he knew above!
>
> In heaven, only one will is accomplished: God's will, which means joy—peace—unity.
>
> Jesus walked the earth having the nostalgia for heaven, for this reason he did everything possible so that "here below" we might live as "there above." This was his final prayer: that they may be one![9]

These writings are rich in elements that we will consider one by one. The unity spoken about is a supernatural unity, paralleled with that of the Trinity. It demands that each person lose his or her self in the heat of divine love in order to allow Christ to live within oneself. Therefore, the product of two or more who unite is not a simple "sum of the parts," but something new (take, for example, chemical combination). It is "Jesus—Oneness." To live this unity concretely means to love one's neighbor to the point of "losing oneself," to the point of cancelling oneself out (refer also to Introduction, B), but only through Christ, who makes persons "dead to themselves" and "alive to grace," is this possible. Therefore, Christ is the one who creates unity and is also its end result.

The following is a writing of 1949 which explains the mystical aspect of this "before and after" of the presence of Christ and which contains other valuable intuitions on unity.

You see, therefore, for him to be present [Jesus in our midst], this is how we must live [love one another as Christ loved us]. But you know that loving in this way means being "other Christs."

Now, for him to be present among us, it is necessary that we already be him beforehand.

But it is a before that is also an after. It is a mystery that can be easily lived, but it is beyond reason.

In fact, we are not perfectly him until he is in our midst.

When he is among us, we are *one* and we are *three*, each equal to the one.

In essence, we can sense when he is present among us: when we feel free, one, full of light. When torrents of living water flow from within us.

What happens between you and me is similar to what happens between the persons of the Trinity.

It is difficult to explain this in human terms.

So try to understand me.

The Holy Spirit is third, after the Father and the Son. He proceeds from both.

Yet he is eternal with the two.

In fact, how can we imagine a Father who generates and loves the Son, if Love is not in him? And how can we imagine a Son who loves if Love is not in him? Yet, [Love] proceeds from the other two and is third (so to speak).

In our own terms we would say that each one of the three is at the same time before and after the other two.

This happens when two are united in the name of Jesus. They must be Jesus in order to have him among them, but they are Jesus when they have him among them. . . .

When we are united and he is present, we are no longer two, but *one*.

In fact, what I say—it is not I who say it, but I, Jesus and you in me. And when you speak, it is not you, but you, Jesus, and I in you. We are a *single Jesus and we are also distinct*: I (with you in me and Jesus), you (with me in you and Jesus), and Jesus among us in whom there are you and I.

His is a mystical presence among us.

He is in the Father; therefore, in him, the two of us are in the Father and we participate in the life of the Trinity.

The trinitarian life flows freely in us, and as we love the others as He has loved us, we bring them to participate in this treasure of divine life.

Or better, they experience in themselves the treasure they had already received when they were engrafted into God through Jesus by way of baptism and the other sacraments.

The novelty of this insight (a practical one) is that not only must we not be, but it is not even possible to be, parasites of Jesus among us, meaning to live comfortably off him passively awaiting his light. In fact, he is not among us when we are not him. It is necessary therefore that we direct all our efforts toward being like him, while still awaiting passively that he might come among us so that we can be him.[10]

This writing takes us immediately back to Chiara's explanation that in supernatural realities, before and after are not to be understood in a temporal sense and therefore can be superimposed—as what happens analogously when we are both active and passive to being Christ.

There is a reference to the grace received at baptism, but this life "flows freely" and is experienced more fully in living with "Jesus in our midst."

In fact, in Jesus who is in our midst, we, united in him, are in the Father and we participate in the trinitarian life. Our life takes on the form of the Trinity ("we are a single Jesus, and we are also distinct"). Here there is an implicit reference to John 17:21 ("I in you," "you in me").

A letter of 1948 speaks more specifically about this reference to John 17:21.

> The important thing is to have as a foundation, means and end—*unity*.
>
> In this unity willed by God, the two souls are fused in *one* and they reappear as *equal and distinct*.
>
> As in the Most Holy Trinity. Jesus wanted it in his testament which is the synthesis of all his thoughts! The thoughts of a God!
>
> "May they be one, as I and you. . . ."[11]

Chiara, in fact, sees the "trinitarian mark" on her work as deriving from Jesus' last prayer.

> In the entire Work of Mary there is the mark of the unity and trinity of God. What gives us this impression is that it stems from the testament of Jesus, where Jesus asks the Father that the unity of people with God and among themselves be similar to the unity between himself and the Father.[12]

She affirms, as seen above, that only God can shape such a unity, therefore Jesus, in asking for it, turned to the Father.[13]

Let's call our attention again to how this unity is repeatedly described as unity and distinction, that of being Jesus individually and collectively.[14] About her 1949 experience Chiara writes:

> We were no longer ourselves, but he in us: he, the divine fire that was consuming our two very different souls into a third soul, his—all fire. So, we were one and three. Jesus. Jesus in him, Jesus in me, Jesus among us. Our dwelling was a ciborium containing one or three Jesus'.[15]

This reflects the life of the Trinity.

> The more we are consumed into one, the more we will acquire the virtues of one another (all that is mine is yours)

in such a way that we will all be *one*, each the other, everyone Jesus. We will be many persons who are equal, yet distinct, because the virtues in us will be clothed by the characteristic virtue that will form our own personality.

We will reflect the Trinity where the Father is distinct from the Son and the Holy Spirit, while containing within himself both the Son and the Holy Spirit. He is equal therefore to the Spirit who contains in himself the Father and the Son, and to the Son who contains in himself both the Father and the Holy Spirit.[16]

In the life of unity, therefore, each comes to acquire the virtue of the other, and contain it within oneself in a similar way in which each of the persons of the Trinity "contains" in oneself the other two. And yet, each of us remains distinct because the virtues in each person are "clothed" by that characteristic virtue that forms one's supernatural personality.

Naturally, the analogy is not perfect, people being limited and finite as they are. Chiara explains:

The union God wants us to have among one another is a unity in distinction. In fact, Jesus could have said, "Where two or three are united in my name, I will fuse them." But he didn't say that. Instead he said, "I will be in the midst of them." This implies unity and distinction.

Human beings are finite and cannot penetrate each other, but God can penetrate each.[17]

Unity between two human persons, therefore, cannot occur as happens in God—an interpenetration. Two persons are one through a third, Jesus, who penetrates both.

A profound writing, again of 1949, describes the life that is lived "in the manner of the Trinity" from another perspective: that of the presence of God, one and triune, in each person. The writing begins by comparing an individual spirituality, through which one searches for God primarily within, to a communitarian spirituality, through which he is sought also in others: "God, who lives in me, who has shaped my soul, and rests therein as Trinity (with the angels and with the saints) also lives in the heart of my neighbors. It's not reasonable to love him only in myself." Chiara continues:

> Therefore my cell (as those intimate with God would say) is us: my heaven is in me, and *as* it is in me it is also in the soul of my neighbors.
>
> Just as I love him in me, recollecting myself in this heaven—when I am alone—I also love him in my neighbors when I am near to them.
>
> I will love then, not silence, but the word (spoken or unspoken), that is, the communication between God in me and God in my neighbor. And if the two heavens meet, there rests a single Trinity where the two are like Father and Son and among them is the Holy Spirit.
>
> We must recollect ourselves also in the presence of our neighbor, not by escaping our neighbors—but rather by recollecting them into our heaven and recollecting ourselves into their heaven.
>
> Since this Trinity abides in human persons, Jesus, the God-man, is present.[18]

Here the indwelling of the Trinity is considered in its dynamic and communitarian dimension. If God in me expresses himself and is received by God in the other, there lies among us a reflection of the same life of the Trinity ("a single Trinity where the two are as Father and Son and among them is the Holy Spirit").

We will take up the role of the Holy Spirit further on.

The last sentence of the above quotation indicates that through the Incarnation, the life of grace in each of us, besides being a divinization, is more specifically a "Christification"; so it is that, in regard to the collective dimension, the life of grace "among us" is more specifically the life of "Christ among us."

Chiara links this "collective mysticism" to Jesus' new commandment: "Love one another as I have loved you" (Jn 15:12). Speaking about this commandment she writes:

> The life we must try to imitate is the life of the Holy Trinity, by loving each other, with the grace of God, in the

way the persons of the Holy Trinity love one another. Living in this manner gives the world the strongest witness of God.[19]

Here is another significant writing that links these aspects together and points out that the new commandment put into practice is a reflection of the life of the Trinity:

> Ours is a mysticism distinctly . . . of the new commandment, the mysticism of the Church, in which the Church is truly Church because she is *unity*, the mystical body, love, because in her circulates the Holy Spirit who makes her the spouse of Christ.
>
> It is the mysticism of Jesus, of a complete Jesus, not of another Jesus, well, yes another Jesus, but one who is complete; the mysticism of *the* Man, not of a man. And Jesus is found where there are two or more; therefore, it is the mysticism of those who love one another as he loved us; the mysticism of a unity of souls who are a reflection, here on earth, of the Trinity above: here on earth, because here below we bear witness to the God-man and here below is the Church.[20]

Explaining the dynamics of trinitarian love Chiara writes:

> Three . . . form the Trinity, yet they are one because love is and is not at the same time. Even when love is not, it is, because it is love. In fact, if I renounce a particular possession of mine and *give it away* (I deprive myself of it—it is not) out of love, *I have love*—therefore *it is*.[21]

This is a very profound text that describes the paradox of the nature of love that "is and is not at the same time," and furthermore, "even when love is not, it is" because it is a total gift of self. This is how it is in God: love is identical with being and simultaneously with the "emptying of self," that is, with the total gift of self.

Chiara applies these same dynamics to our way of loving, affirming that "whether in our relationship with God or with our neighbors, we must be and not be at the same time . . . by being love."[22] Therefore, "it is the dynamics of the Holy Trinity, in which the Father eternally generates the Son and we would say that he empties himself. But no! Precisely because he generates the Son, he gives his entire self: he is."[23]

Chiara sees this kind of relationship as intrinsic in the human race, for it was created in the image of God.

> I felt that I was created as a gift for the person next to me, and the person next to me was created by God as a gift for me. As the Father in the Trinity is everything for the Son and the Son is everything for the Father.[24]

So, in this section we wanted to show how life with Jesus in our midst reflects the life of the Trinity. It is a life of unity, that strengthens at the same time the presence of Jesus in each one, and therefore in this life there is also distinction. It is the life of reciprocal love, patterned on the Trinity.

It has been mentioned also that this is the mysticism of the Church as the mystical body. We'll come back to this point in the next chapter. For now, as a conclusion to this part, let's take a look at a very unique description which links these elements together. After having spoken of Jesus in our midst, Chiara explains how the mystical body can be viewed from different angles: for example, through its various members who are joined to one another, or through "him who binds the members together." She continues:

> Now let's imagine . . . all these members are joined in such a way that there is a knot that binds each member with the other. This Christ who is among the members is Christ in the members, who, having practically assumed our persons, makes it so that it is no longer we who live, but Christ who lives in us.
>
> Now, if we take all these knots together (the knots being Christ among all the different members, who is Christ himself, the head of the mystical body), one would see a sort of net take shape. This net is the "Mystical Christ" in the mystical body of Christ: this is . . . *agape*.
>
> Why is this so? It is because *agape* means love, a love that binds. The knot is really more than just a knot, and more than a relationship, it is the love that we are. It is the mystical body seen not from the angle of its singular members, but from the one who binds them together.[25]

Chiara relies on the help of images to describe the mystical body, considered in its aspect of unity, of "love that binds," which is at the same time Christ in us and among us.

But we know that whether it is in the mystical body or in the Trinity, the bond of unity is the Holy Spirit. Let's then consider the particular aspect of the relation between the Holy Spirit and Jesus in our midst, which emerges from Chiara's thought.

B. JESUS IN OUR MIDST AND THE HOLY SPIRIT

While amply underlining the christological aspect of the mystical body, Chiara is well aware of the role of the Holy Spirit as the bond of unity.[26] The writing of November 6, 1949, cited earlier, spoke of the Holy Spirit "among" two souls that live the spirituality of unity.[27]

It is he who moves about among the members of the mystical body and makes them one, he who makes them other Christs.

> Our mysticism presupposes at least two souls become God, among whom the Holy Spirit truly moves about . . . that is, a third, God that consumes them into one, into a single God. "As I and you," Jesus tells the Father. Then and only then are the two Jesus.[28]

Said in another way, the Holy Spirit, as in the Trinity, is the relationship among us.

> So is it that the relationship between the one who is responsible of the focolare center, and the other Focolarini, is the Holy Spirit, which is the same relationship that exists among the persons in the Trinity ("Father, may they be one, as I and you").[29]

When we are bound together, we form a single Jesus. Chiara cites the example of the focolare center "where the Focolarini together with the one responsible for their household are consumed into one through the Holy Spirit that binds them forming a single Jesus."[30]

Therefore, we become Jesus, singularly and together, with Jesus in our midst, through the work of the Holy Spirit.[31]

From a certain standpoint, Jesus in our midst and the Holy Spirit which moves about among us can be identified with one another. We have already established, from the writings cited thus far, that both Jesus in our midst and the Holy Spirit are called "bonds of unity." Speaking to a group within the Focolare, Chiara specifically said: "In the mystical body of Christ, the members of the body are bound together by the Holy Spirit or by Jesus in their midst; it's the same thing." She continued explaining, "because the spirit of Jesus is the Holy Spirit."[32]

More in particular, Jesus in our midst is identified with the Holy Spirit, the soul of the mystical body. Perhaps this idea was confirmed for Chiara after a conversation with Fr. Martegani in 1961.[33] In the contents of that meeting, we find it stated in the following terms.

> What I feel I must bring (in circles outside of the Church) is the presence of the soul of the Church among us. I don't even know how to define it because Jesus in the midst of us and the Holy Spirit, the soul of the Church are one, they coincide with one another.[34]

However, already a few months prior to that meeting she had said: "True, the bond that lies between us is Jesus in our midst, but it is also the Holy Spirit, because he is the soul of the mystical body. It is the same thing."[35]

This is why in speaking of the focolare center where "there is Jesus in the midst," we can find a reference to Pentecost[36] and to the early Christian communities where "there flowed the breath of the Holy Spirit."[37]

However, if from one standpoint, Jesus in our midst and the Holy Spirit, which moves about among us, are identified with one another, Chiara explains also in what way they are not. To Fr. Veuthey, who had asked her why Jesus had said "Where two or more are gathered together in my name, there am I in the midst of them" and not "there is my spirit," she responded:

> Just as Jesus said: "Saul, Saul, why do you persecute me?" for he saw himself in those Christians, because his mystical

body is he himself, he also said, "Where two or more are gathered together in my name there am I." Therefore, Jesus' presence in our midst, if we are two or more united, means that we are the human part of Christ, while the divine part is his Spirit present in us through grace, as is commonly understood, and this special divine grace which is his presence.[38]

On another occasion Chiara, in agreement with the point of view of Fr. Foresi, the Focolare's co-president, states that while the gifts of the Spirit go beyond socio-cultural conditions, there still remains a certain link between them. The presence, therefore, of Jesus in our midst is limited and conditioned by the persons who compose it, by the humanity that they lend to Jesus in their midst. Proposing the example of the difference of Jesus in the midst there could be among children and among adults Chiara adds, "I can affirm that culture, age, an era in time, can give different appearances to Jesus in our midst."[39]

Finally, let's call back to mind another statement: Jesus in our midst brings the Holy Spirit. A writing of 1950 makes this affirmation: "Jesus is among us, and with him is the Holy Spirit who fills us with his gifts."[40] Chiara did not speak much further on this, but in 1975, when studying the presence of Jesus in the midst in the Fathers of the Church, she notes that Origen lists three gifts that God grants to those who are united: Jesus in their midst, the Holy Spirit, and that of attaining whatever they ask for. Commenting further she affirms, "Jesus in our midst, therefore, brings the Holy Spirit with him."[41]

So we see that numerous relationships emerge between Jesus in our midst and the Holy Spirit. It is the Holy Spirit who makes us one, and therefore creates the premises for Jesus in our midst. The Holy Spirit is the bond of unity and therefore, under this aspect, he is in a certain way identified with Jesus in our midst. The Holy Spirit is a gift of Jesus and therefore, from this standpoint, the result of Jesus in our midst. It is a before, a together, and an after, that as we have seen before, are not contradictory in the mystical life.

From the preceding writings, we have already singled out references to the concept of self-denial as linked to the conditions for having the presence of Jesus in our midst, and also, on occasion, to the expression Jesus forsaken. It is an expression which recalls the moment Jesus cried out on the cross, "My God, my God, why have you forsaken me" (Mt 27:46). The richness that lies here, including our participation in this moment of Jesus' life is too broad to cover at great length in this particular study. In fact, along with Jesus in our midst, Jesus forsaken is another cardinal point of Chiara's spirituality.

In this section we will make only a few references to the relationship between Jesus forsaken and Jesus in our midst. To begin with, we will cite this brief explanation of Jesus forsaken, referring to other writings for greater depth.[42]

> Another idea and driving force of our movement cannot but be the cross: the consideration and the application in the life of individuals and of the Focolare itself of the passion and death of Jesus.
>
> Through a given circumstance, God had drawn our attention to a particular aspect of this mystery: *the abandonment of Jesus*, when "toward mid-afternoon Jesus cried out in a loud tone, 'My God, my God, why have you forsaken me?'" (Mt 27:46). It is the culmination of his sufferings, his interior passion, his darkest night.
>
> It is the drama of a God who cries, "My God, why have you forsaken me? . . ."
>
> It is the infinite mystery, the abysmal agony that Jesus experienced as a man and which gives the measure of his love for the human race, in that he wanted to take upon himself the separation that kept it far from its Father, he wanted to fill in this gap.
>
> The Focolare is rich in experience that demonstrates how every human suffering is contained in this particular suffering of Jesus.

71

Are not the anguished, the lonely, the disheartened, the disillusioned, the fallen, the weak . . . similar to him? Is he not an image of every painful division between people, between churches, between portions of humanity that hold contrasting ideologies? Is not the atheistic, secularized world, fallen into every kind of aberration a figure of Jesus who loses, so to speak, his sense of God, of Jesus who made himself "sin" for us?

Through loving Jesus forsaken, a Christian finds the reason and strength not to run away from these evils and divisions, but to accept them for him and to consume them and thus offer to them a personal remedy.

Here then, is Jesus forsaken, the key to unity, the secret to every renewal.[43]

The relationship between the cross and unity for Chiara can be traced back to the beginning of 1945, that is, even before the specific "discovery" of Jesus in their midst in a letter already quoted in part in the introduction.

I ask the Eternal Father, in the name of Jesus, for the grace to hasten the hour in which all of you may be one, with one heart, one will, one thought.

Whose?

That of Jesus crucified!

Then, drawn to the cross (which will draw all to himself) you will work toward fusing your little community into a solid block, and thus give to God the greatest glory! God will live among you; you will sense his presence; you will enjoy his presence; he will give you his light; he will inflame you with his love! To come to this point however, you must devote yourselves to *him crucified*.[44]

Love for Jesus crucified is seen here as essential for unity and therefore, for the presence of God in the community. In the following years this connection becomes ever clearer still.

Unity is a utopia if it is not formed by souls who immolate themselves in order to become *one*.

Even here, the great secret of souls who are apostles of unity is Jesus forsaken! Those who search for him find *unity*. Those who do not love him become disheartened, and sterile in *unity* which—otherwise—is always fruitful in souls.[45]

Chiara will explain then how "making ourselves one with our neighbor" requires this particular love for Jesus forsaken.

To welcome into ourselves the one who is everything, we must, like Jesus forsaken, become nothing. On a blank sheet, anyone can write ... We must in everyone's regard be disposed to learn, to truly know that there is [something] to learn. Only the one who is nothing can welcome into oneself everything, and furthermore, hold onto everything in unity. We must *be nothing* (Jesus forsaken) in the presence of each of our neighbors in order to embrace Jesus in him or her.[46]

Here is another clarification.

Jesus forsaken is the model for those who must establish unity with their neighbors. In fact, I cannot enter in another spirit if I am rich of my own. To love my neighbors I must constantly be poor of spirit so as to not possess anything but love. Love is being empty of self. Jesus forsaken is the perfect model for one who is poor in spirit: he is so poor that he does not even have God, so to speak. He does not sense his presence.[47]

This strong link between Jesus forsaken and unity has been included in the statutes [an earlier draft] of the Work of Mary under article 10, where love for the cross is spoken of as a necessary condition for unity:

The life of union among the faithful, within the limits of a well-ordered and evangelical charity, will require in its members a very particular love for the cross, in particular for Jesus in the mystery of his passion. [It is he who is] the divine model for all those who desire to collaborate toward the union of people with God and among one another. He is the apex of physical deprivation, but more specially, interior deprivation, the necessary condition for every effort toward union animated by supernatural motives.[48]

Describing this interior deprivation Chiara also says:

> The Focolarino acts in this way because our life requires that *we leave God for God*. This detachment (one of the many of our life which reminds us of Jesus forsaken) is one of the conditions for unity in the focolare center, whose members must be of one heart and one soul.[49]

Jesus forsaken is also said to be the means for having Jesus in our midst. Chiara speaks of this "relationship of the means to the end," stating that "Jesus forsaken is the necessary means to arrive at Jesus in our midst." And clarifying further, "as Jesus in his abandonment has redeemed humanity, in the sense that he reunited us his children to the Father (he was the means that brought about unity), so too Jesus forsaken, when loved, brings about Jesus in our midst."[50]

There are different applications that can be derived from the relationship between Jesus forsaken and Jesus in our midst. First of all, Jesus forsaken makes us perfect in unity, which is the condition for having the presence of Jesus in our midst. In fact, love for Jesus forsaken fosters a personal union with God, and therefore, the more each person is "full of God," the more one will be "perfect in unity." Here is how Chiara explains it.

> Jesus forsaken, in fact, was the one who was making us perfect in unity. In his testament Jesus had said, "I living in them, you living in me—that their unity may be complete" (Jn 17:23).
>
> If Jesus was in me, if Jesus was in the other person, if Jesus was in everyone, in that moment we would have been perfect in unity.
>
> However—I repeat—so that Jesus might be in us we had to love Jesus forsaken in all the suffering, emptiness, failures, and sadness that life brings.
>
> This union filled us with God, so much so, that when we met each other, we recognized ourselves in each other because

it was God in me, God in my neighbor, and God in everyone. Only then did we feel we were brothers and sisters.[51]

Jesus forsaken is also the means to reconstruct unity that was broken because of a lack in charity. Describing the discomfort and darkness that was experienced when the "sun" of Jesus in their midst had set, Chiara continues:

> In these moments, only the thought of him, abandoned in deepest spiritual darkness, gave us hope that all was not lost, that ours was a suffering that could be pleasing to God if offered to him with love. And so we would try to do this. Then we would set about courageously trying to restore unity among ourselves. . . .
>
> Then the sunshine would return to our little community, the sunshine of Jesus' presence among those who are united in his name.[52]

On another occasion she explains how, when there is a disunity caused by someone else, love for Jesus forsaken in oneself and in the others leads the way back to unity.

> Those who live in the focolare centers, when hurt at being abandoned by another, come to an understanding of being in a state of soul similar to his [Jesus forsaken] and feel not only prompted to rejoice in that suffering, but see in the other person another Jesus forsaken to console and to love. Love reestablishes unity.[53]

Finally, we note how Chiara speaks of a "dwelling together" with Jesus forsaken "through the practice of the negative virtues,"[54] which, as we have seen above, are also required for maintaining the presence of Jesus in our midst.[55] She also adds, "so that we might refine our spirits always more, and contemplate, not the light, but the one who is the giver of light." Concluding, she says, "in this way Jesus' presence in our midst will be always greater, and he will do marvelous things."[56]

Therefore, Jesus forsaken is the means for having Jesus in our midst. But there is also an inverse effect. When Jesus is in our midst we feel new ardor in our choice of Jesus forsaken.

If we need Jesus in our midst in order to be enlightened and to be fulfilled as individuals and as a community, we must however not forget that it is not he whom we have espoused, but rather, Jesus forsaken.

Among the many effects of Jesus in our midst, there is also that of being a springboard for renewing in us the desire and the ardor, and let's say it—from a human standpoint—the madness to go out again to encounter Jesus forsaken.[57]

In this present chapter we have considered the presence of Jesus in our midst and its relationship with the life of unity and the trinitarian life, with the Holy Spirit, and with Jesus forsaken. We will conclude with a writing of 1951, wherein Chiara explains the life of the mystical body of Christ, linking these various elements together. This will serve as a summary of what has been said thus far. The next chapter will deal with the ecclesiological aspects of Jesus in our midst.

Chiara begins this writing by quoting Acts of the Apostles 9:4 and Matthew 25:35 and 40 in order to highlight the presence of Jesus in each Christian. She then proceeds:

All Christians therefore are one because the One Christ lives in all of them: they are *identified* with Christ.

Jesus of Nazareth is the head of all these members and with them forms a single body: the mystical body.

The spirit of Jesus is the soul of this body, the principle of unity. In fact, his spirit, which is the Holy Spirit, lives in everyone according to Leo XIII, "We have said it all when we say that Christ is the head of the Church, the Holy Spirit is her soul" (*Divinum illud, A.A.S.* XXIX, p. 650).

Because Christ lives in everyone, we are all one with the head and one among ourselves.

Christ is also the bond among us: "For where two or three are gathered together in my name, there am I in the midst of them" (Mt 18:20).

Since Christ is in us his Spirit is in us and the Father is in us. Therefore, letting Christ live in us, the Holy Trinity lives in us.

And we, in living Christ, have access to the Father, just as, in living Christ we are filled with his Spirit.

There are certain conditions required for this to happen: to be incorporated in him through baptism, which is the baptism of the Spirit, and to correspond to this gift. Without our own correspondence, we cannot share in this one Spirit, which makes us one with Christ and with the Father, and one among ourselves.

Christ lives in us if we live like Christ, if we make his words our own, if we observe his commands. . . .

But all commandments can be reduced to one: to love. . . .

The Christian therefore responds to grace by loving. By loving, the Christian is in God, and therefore is another Jesus.

But we must love as Jesus loved. Only by being crucified with Christ are we alive with the life of Christ.

The range of sufferings that the Christian must bear out of love for Christ in one's neighbor is infinite, but no suffering ever exceeds that of Jesus forsaken; he remains as the eternal and unattainable model . . .

Jesus' new commandment, the one dearest to his heart was *reciprocal* love in the measure he loved us. "I give you a new commandment: love one another; just as I have loved you" (Jn 13:34).

In fact he wanted to bring to earth the life of the Holy Trinity.

And if two "other Christs" love one another as he loved us, it is really God who loves God and among the two is the Holy Spirit, just as the Holy Spirit is among the Father and the Son.

This is the reciprocal love that we want to live in the focolare centers. With reciprocal love, the Focolarini will remain as living members of the mystical body . . .

The Focolarini, therefore, in their love for one another become another Christ. Because they love one another they are one with the head and they can become always more united with him. The Focolarini therefore want to be united among one another so as to be united to their head. For the

Focolarini, the way that leads to Christ the head is Christ the member.[58]

This writing tells us that the unity spoken about in the preceding pages as precondition and effect of the life of Jesus in our midst is, fundamentally, the life of the mystical body. This life which we receive through the Holy Spirit makes each one another Christ. This implies, besides baptism, a "response to this gift" by living as Christ, and by loving as he loved us, to its extreme measure, Jesus forsaken. The more we love as he loved, the more we become another him. And if our love is reciprocal, our life reflects the life of the Trinity, wherein the Holy Spirit is the bond of unity.

In the following chapter, we will examine the various ecclesiological aspects of the presence of Jesus in our midst found in Chiara's writings, and at the same time, its social dimensions.

Chapter 3

ECCLESIOLOGICAL AND
SOCIOLOGICAL ASPECTS OF
JESUS IN OUR MIDST

A. THE ECCLESIOLOGICAL DIMENSION OF JESUS IN OUR MIDST

The spirituality of unity, of Jesus in our midst, was born in the Church and would not have meaning if it were detached from the Church. In fact, since the beginning, the importance of "engrafting" with the hierarchical Church has always been underlined. Furthermore, one of the effects which the life of Jesus in our midst had brought was a new understanding and appreciation for the dogma, the sacraments, and the life of the Church in its entirety. Further still, experience showed that living with Jesus in our midst makes us become Church, and thus revealed its intrinsic ecclesiological dimension.

The importance of being engrafted into the hierarchical Church

The fact that Chiara so early on presented herself, along with her companions, to the bishop of Trent, ready to discontinue everything should he give the word, bears witness to the awareness that what had been born belonged to the Church and therefore had to be submitted to its leaders in its entirety. We will not go further into detail on this point, though much documentation can be found in the history of the life of Chiara and the movement she founded.[1] We'll limit ourselves to viewing how she links this disposition to Jesus in our midst. In 1950 she writes:

Only Jesus among us was our master, father and guide. In order to walk in the light it was enough to have him, yet not even him would we have wanted had the Church not approved of this life of ours. For this reason the light that came from the presence of Jesus among us was subjected to the one who represented the Church to us. For us there was no Christ without the Church.

But perhaps it was for this unconditional and adamant subjection that we always had the sensation that the spirit which moved about among us was in perfect tune with the spirit of the Mother Church. One confirmed the other, and vice versa.[2]

In 1961, when speaking with Fr. Martegani, a Jesuit appointed by the Holy See to assist in the drafting of the Focolare's statutes, Chiara grasped another aspect. The presence of Jesus in a small community is the very same presence that is in the entire Church; that is, the presence of Jesus as head of the whole Church, and this is because the former is engrafted into the whole Church as "branches united to the vine."[3] As we will see further on, this gives us the possibility of "being Church" everywhere.

Jesus in our midst draws us to understand and to love the Church

We have noted above that one of the effects of the presence of Jesus in our midst is light, which gives a clearer understanding of divine realities.[4] Attributed to his presence, from the very beginning, was a new understanding and love for the mystery of the Church. Also of great importance was the effect of better comprehending the words of the Holy Father and the bishops. It was as if "their teachings" said Chiara, "had found an echo in our hearts."[5]

Even the dogmas of faith, Chiara continues, "acquired the flavor of true realities" and "seemed less obscure to us. While remaining mysteries, they were nonetheless more understood."[6]

We also find the expressions of having a "sense of the Church, in its hierarchy and its teaching," "a deep understanding of the Church," and "the feeling of being one with the Church."[7]

All this, due to the presence of Jesus in our midst. Explaining this phenomenon, Chiara says, "It's logical! Because Christ is the spouse of the Church. The Church is the spouse of Christ."[8] And then: "In exposing ourselves to fire, we become fire. By having Jesus in our midst, we become other Christs, and since Christ loves the Church, we too will acquire a passion for the Church."[9] Through love, a new understanding is born, as she explained on another occasion, "We loved the Church, therefore everything pertaining to it took on new life for us; we understood the sacraments as never before. The dogmas became clearer. Our souls absorbed the Christian doctrine."[10]

Jesus in our midst makes us Church

We have briefly mentioned above how life with Jesus in our midst is the life of the mystical body in action.[11] "The Lord reopened the mystery of the Church for us" Chiara tells, "that is, he led us to understand what it means to be Church and to live it with greater awareness. He unveiled a spirituality, which is the spirituality of the mystical body, the spirituality of the Church."[12]

A writing of 1950 bears this in mind. It begins by speaking about the new commandment and Jesus' last prayer, "May they all be one." It continues:

> We live (this prayer) in the way we understand it. We saw it as the synthesis of the entire gospel, so complete a synthesis as to produce the most desired effect: the fullness of the life of the Church, of the mystical body, where the members live so fully the life of Jesus as to become other Christs. This happens not only through the life of grace that lies within them, and makes them sharers of the divine life, but also because this way of life is so full and overflowing as to be poured over and over onto others (while still able to reach an always greater fullness). Through Jesus in our midst (who is present where two or more . . .) this life forms everyone into one body, one soul, one Jesus.[13]

The writing continues:

> Today I read part of the *Mystici Corporis*, born from the
> heart of Christ's vicar on earth in 1943, the year in which the
> Lord enlightened the first Focolarine about our Ideal.
>
> And our Ideal . . . is nothing but a divine infusion so that
> the mystical body, the Church that is, might live her divine
> life to the full. The Focolarini were born for this, that in the
> unity of two or more . . . they might bring Jesus among the
> faithful and make of the faithful, other Christs, living and
> healthy members of the mystical body.[14]

It is a question, therefore, of living the life of the Church to the
full. Addressing a group of priests in 1969 Chiara spoke of Jesus
present in liturgical celebrations. "However, the effect would be
greater if the faithful, together with the priest, loved one another.
The presence of Jesus would be fuller and richer in graces, and
would extend to everyone."[15]

In 1975, encouraged by a statement of Pope Paul VI on Jesus in
our midst, which she quoted later in her book, Chiara felt urged to
state clearly that where there is a lack in the fullness of this life of
reciprocal love, the Church is not as Christ intended it to be.

> I saw that the pope speaks very clearly on this subject. It
> is a rather serious thing for the pope to say that there is no
> true Church where Jesus in its midst is lacking because the
> cement that would unite the members of the mystical body
> together is lacking. . . .
>
> Let's understand each other well concerning the word
> "true." I'm not talking about heresy: it's just not the Church
> that Christ had intended . . . Therefore, [those faithful] are
> potentially in the full beauty of the Church; they are Church,
> but they are like this room with the lights out. The room is
> here, but you cannot see it. So too, the Church is present, but
> you cannot see it.[16]

Jesus in our midst not only gives fullness to ecclesial life in its
liturgical forms, but, if we are linked as we should be in the
hierarchically constituted Church, Jesus in our midst makes us

"Church," a "little Church," wherever we are, even if we are just two or three. Speaking about the beginning of the Focolare, Chiara says: "There in Trent we began to understand the mystery of the Church, since we ourselves were living as a little Church."[17] And during that period of illumination, what surfaced was a mystical understanding of this intrinsic ecclesiological dimension. "The Lord had led us to understand that we were Church," Chiara says. "The handful of persons that the Lord had selected to manifest himself became, at a certain moment, Church."[18]

It is the mystery of the local Church viewed at its most essential level, "two or more" united in supernatural love. We see this concept developed by Chiara in a meditation wherein she cites a confirmation in Odo Casel.

> The Council and the pope stress this several times: the community united like a family in the name of the Lord enjoys his presence. We are speaking of the kind of brotherhood that makes us Church, as Odo Casel points out, "It is not that the single Church breaks up into a plurality of different communities, nor does the multiplicity of different communions united together form the single Church. The Church is only *one*, wherever it appears, it is all entire and undivided, even where only two or three are gathered in the name of Christ." Now maybe we Christians are not always fully aware of this extraordinary possibility.[19]

In another meditation Chiara explains the relationship between the local and universal Church going back to the mystery of the Trinity. After underlining the dual necessity that the local Churches be places of communion among the members, and of unity with the pope, she continues:

> This dual stance of deep union among the members and with Rome makes it possible, through the mystery of the mystical body patterned on the Most Holy Trinity, that in any location where there is a Church, in that place there is also *the* Church.
>
> Now if this holds true for the Churches instituted by Christ founded on the apostles, so much the more is it a must for

every spontaneous group or movement that has risen or will rise up among the faithful.

If this happens we will be immersed in the full flowering of Spring and we will note how, even in the smallest group of Christians, what St. Bonaventure said hold's true: "Where two or three are united in the name of Christ, there is the Church."[20]

In her 1976 publication on Jesus in our midst, Chiara cites some of the Fathers of the Church who confirm this concept. Here is one comment of hers.

We have always liked the saying of Tertullian: "Where three [are gathered together], even if they are laypersons, there is the Church."

Yes, because we are often a small group united and juridically grafted onto the entire Church of Christ.

Therefore, even if we are few, we are Church, the living Church, through the presence of Jesus among us.[21]

In conclusion, we present this final concept: Jesus in our midst is capable of generating churches. Making reference to the experience of a group of the Focolare at Fontem, in Africa, Chiara explains:

Since we are Church, we are capable of generating churches. This is what happens with missionaries who go to some far-off place that has not yet been evangelized and found a church, the local church.

This is what happened with us, too, in Fontem (West Cameroon, Africa), for example, where the first two or three Focolarini, though they were laymen, succeeded in building up a parish which is an integral part of the diocese of Buea, because Christ was among them.[22]

Logically, in emphasizing this point, there is no intention of denying the role of the priest and the central importance of the eucharist, etc. in the life of the parish, but rather of underlining the role of Jesus in our midst in generating this life.

Before touching upon the wide topic of ecumenism and its significant relationship to Jesus in our midst, we will gather a few specific comments Chiara makes in linking the presence of Jesus in our midst to the eucharist, the religious orders, the priesthood, and the Council.

Jesus in our midst and the eucharist

Two lines are clearly drawn: the eucharist is directed toward establishing the presence of Jesus in our midst; and Jesus in our midst substitutes for it where it is not possible to receive the eucharist.

a) The eucharist is directed toward Jesus in our midst

To the specific question on the relationship between Jesus in our midst and Jesus in the eucharist, Chiara responds that "Jesus in the eucharist is a function of Jesus in our midst."[23] Elsewhere she affirms that it is the "means for having Jesus in our midst."[24]

This is logical if we consider the relationship of the eucharist with unity, which in 1950 Chiara had already expressed in these terms: "We cannot understand unity without the sacrament of unity, the one thing that makes everybody one, one single body."[25] Also, in her book on the eucharist Chiara speaks of a "marvelous intertwining between the eucharist and the ideal of unity"[26] and dedicates a chapter on "The eucharist and communion among brothers and sisters."[27] A page of her diary affirms:

> Jesus in our midst does not substitute for Jesus in the eucharist, but is nourished by him. . . . Generally, unity for us is unthinkable without Jesus in the eucharist; he is the bond of unity.[28]

Finally, let's recall that, while the eucharist can be received once a day, we can live with Jesus in our midst in every moment of the day. A prayer of Chiara reads:

> Nourish us, O Lord, each morning by means of your flesh, but make us so docile as to hasten the hour in which you can nourish all the moments of our life with your presence among us.[29]

b) Jesus in our midst substitutes for the eucharist when it is unavailable

Still another concept is that in situations where it is impossible to receive the eucharist Jesus in the midst can be its substitute. A good example would be in countries where religious persecution exists. At one point Chiara had noted, "Behind the iron curtain Jesus in the midst substitutes for the eucharist by necessity, when it is impossible to receive it." And she continued, "Where there is no possibility to receive communion, no possibility to go to church, for example in places where the Church is nonexistent or has been destroyed, we can still live the Church by establishing the presence of Jesus in our midst."[30]

In the same way Jesus in our midst can be our bond of unity with our brothers and sisters of other Christian confessions with whom we cannot yet share the eucharist. We will speak further about this in the next section on ecumenism.[31]

Jesus in our midst in religious orders and among priests

In the "Commentary on the Rule" dated 1958 we find a description, relating to the Focolare, of a certain "Priests and Religious League" which

> . . . wishes to create a lively current of unity in charity on the part of priests and men and women religious with the pope, the bishops and their superiors, so that with growing intensity, the testament of Jesus can be fulfilled in the ecclesiastical circles.[32]

Within time these three groups of the league (men religious, women religious, and priests) became distinct branches.

In speaking of the presence of Jesus in the midst established among religious of different orders Chiara affirms:

When Jesus said, "Where two or three are gathered together in my name, there am I in the midst of them" (Mt 18:20), he had certainly meant this to include where a Benedictine and a Franciscan, or a Carmelite and a Passionist, or a Jesuit and a Dominican were united in his name. And if he were in their midst, their encounters would make the Benedictine a better Benedictine, the Franciscan a better Franciscan, and so on.[33]

This last effect can be better understood if we consider what Jesus in our midst can bring to religious orders in general.

Jesus in our midst helps the religious to better understand their own founders who were inspired by God himself, by Jesus himself, to better understand their rules which were confirmed by the Church wherein Christ lives, to better understand their brothers and sisters and their superiors with whom, on the strength of this spirit, they can be united. Because they understand their rule better, they live it better . . . they unite themselves with their founder in heaven.[34]

Therefore, we see a dual dimension of Jesus in our midst. One is within the order itself and the other is among the members of different orders. In fact, when explaining to a group of women religious their particular resemblance to Mary, due to their being women, consecrated, and mothers of Christ in other souls, Chiara adds, "and now, with this Ideal, [you are] mothers because you generate the spiritual presence of Jesus among you, in your homes, in your orders and even among the various orders."[35]

For this reason, after examining the fifteenth chapter of the conciliar decree on the renewal of religious life, wherein the passage of Matthew 18:20 is cited, Chiara commented:

When we read this passage, we understand why the Work of Mary had to give birth to its branch of men and women religious. The charism God gave us is brimming over with these ideas, with these truths. This charism could be of help to many religious who might not know how to put the words of the Council into practice, or who, in times of religious crises like these, might no longer understand the meaning of religious life.[36]

In regard to the priests instead, Chiara speaks of a particular mark of Jesus in the midst that they establish among themselves, "that atmosphere which can be created only where persons of the priestly charism are united with one another."[37] To the specific question "What is the particular mark of the focolare center of priests?" she responds, "I would see it as a cenacle focolare center, an Emmaus focolare center let's say, because of the presence of Jesus the priest, Jesus in the midst as priest."[38]

Jesus in our midst and the Council

In reviewing the Fathers of the Church, Chiara realizes that they often cite Matthew 18:20 in order to give evidence for the presence of Jesus in the Councils, and comments:

The Fathers firmly maintain that Jesus is present in the midst of the bishops in council. As a result, the Council becomes like a great hearth (*focolare*) of the Church, where Jesus extends his light abundantly in order to enlighten the centuries ahead.[39]

In this same context, she also cites a passage from Congar, already mentioned in a previous section. Congar sees in the Council "a certain structure to which the Lord freely united his presence with a formal promise," a promise that was formulated in the verses of Matthew 28:20 and 18:20.[40]

Besides the consideration of Jesus in our midst as an underlying presence in the various Councils, Chiara examines this concept as it appears in conciliar documents, especially those of Vatican II, where after many years it clearly reemerges.[41] Characteristic of Chiara's research is the spirit with which she examines these texts, as she says, "it is of greatest importance to see whether the charism that moves us is in harmony with the spirit of the entire present-day Church."[42] Having discovered this consonance she exclaims, "Here we would want to stop and praise God for having led us. . . . Is it not evident that it is Jesus in our midst who leads us on, the same Jesus who presided over the recent Council?"[43]

In a previous diary, she also mentions having noted this same consonance.

> Wherever he (Jesus in our midst) is found, there lives the Church in the new countenance the Council has given her: whether among the youth, in the religious orders, in the parish movement, or in the various centers and works of the Focolare. And all is alive and vibrant while carrying, by means of his presence—linked to thousands of factors of unity with authorities, the magisterium, with all of humanity—the fragrance of that infallibility the Council attributes to the people of God.[44]

Lastly, we'll give just a brief mention to the escatological character of the Councils which Chiara sees as having "no other structure than that the Fathers must be in agreement, that they must love one another, and that Jesus in their midst enlightens and guides them."[45] Here what "appears is more the Church triumphant than the Church militant because in the Church militant we need the hierarchy, the sacraments . . . in the Church triumphant the Lamb of God will be in the midst of his people."[46]

C. JESUS IN OUR MIDST AND ECUMENISM

The relationship of the Focolare with members of other Christian Churches and denominations came to light in spontaneous fashion, beginning in 1960 with a casual encounter with a group of German Evangelicals.[47] But already in a letter of 1948 we find the principle that will animate the spirit of ecumenism that would follow.

> Never depart from one another without having first understood one another. Unity before all else! In everything! Discussions are worth very little, even when centered on the holiest of topics, if they do not give life to Jesus among us, who loved us so much that he gave us *everything*.[48]

Similarly, in 1965, in an introduction prepared for a group of Christians of various churches who had come to Rome to become more familiar with the spirit of the Focolare, she said:

> We are not here to get involved in polemics (this is not a meeting for theologians) even though we must seek the truth in charity.
>
> We are not even here in order to pray, even though we will pray both individually and together.
>
> We are here to love.
>
> And our love will have to be so ardent, so purified by the constant crucifixion of our egos that those who see us will be able to say: there is no Catholic, Lutheran, Anglican, or Orthodox. All are *one* in Christ the Lord. . . .
>
> Then he will spiritually come among us and see for himself how beautiful and joyous it is when brothers and sisters come together. Day by day, hour by hour he will guide us with his suggestions. He will direct the course of the meeting himself. There is no one else whom we must rely upon.[49]

In regard to this possibility of having Jesus in the midst of Catholics and other Christians Chiara tells of the first time she went to meet a group of Evangelicals in Germany. Prior to her trip she was a bit perplexed: "Would there or would there not be Jesus in our midst?" She reasoned: "If they are in God's grace and are ready to give their lives for us, even though they are not Catholic there should still in some way be Jesus in our midst." Before leaving, however, she wanted a confirmation and asked Bishop Vanni, "Can we hold any hope of having Jesus in our midst with Christians of other churches?" His answer, as Chiara reported: "Certainly, my daughter. In some way he is present." It was the first stone set into place for the long ecumenical experience that was to follow.[50]

After that moment Chiara was heard to say on a number of occasions: "Jesus in our midst . . . for me is the foundation stone of ecumenism,"[51] "this is our ecumenical key," "our ecumenism is Jesus in our midst."[52]

In fact, in order to have Jesus in our midst it is necessary to live the new commandment of love, and "the new commandment can be put into practice also between Catholics and Anglicans, between Catholics and Lutherans . . . not only *it can be*, it *must be*."[53]

In 1970, speaking to a group from the Reformed Church Chiara said:

> Let's reach ever greater depths in knowledge and charity, ready to die for one another, to put our own ideas aside, and to learn how to listen to one another, to carry the burdens of one another, to praise what is beautiful in the other. In this way we will gain full entrance into the ecumenical movement that the Holy Spirit . . . desires.[54]

Ecumenism, the eucharist, and Jesus in our midst

Here are some statements of Chiara on these three points.

> Jesus in our midst is a formidable help in building a vital ecumenism. In fact, since we Catholics are not yet able to be united in the eucharist with other Christian Churches and denominations, we can still be united, when the necessary conditions are met, by Jesus present among two or more.[55]

In regard to the necessity of having first the presence of Jesus among us prior to the possibility of intercommunion, Chiara gives the following explanation to a group from the Reformed Church.

> The gospel says that if your brother or sister has something against you, leave your gift at the altar, go first to reconcile yourself with him or her and then offer your gift at the altar.
> Now, I have nothing against you, and I think that neither have you anything against me. However, we do feel that we consciously bear the heredity of those who have made some errors. Errors are never one-sided. Even if our fathers and mothers have not reconciled with one another, we must be reconciled amongst ourselves. We must return to unity ourselves. So I say, let's take a little step back and leave our gifts at the altar, and go and be reconciled with our brothers and

sisters. Then, one day, we will arrive at sharing the one communion. . . . We have to work this division out and the only one capable of doing it is Jesus in our midst. . . . Therefore, the one thing left to do for now, if we cannot receive the body and blood of Christ together, is to receive Jesus spiritually present in our midst.[56]

Chiara, however, still points toward the day in which there will be a sharing in the eucharistic communion. The eucharist will be the crowning of that unity which was reestablished through Jesus in the midst.

What is it that makes us brothers and sisters, what is it that unites us? On the supernatural plane it is the eucharist, the bond of unity, and if the eucharist is not available, it is Jesus in our midst. This is the core of ecumenism. Why? Because it unites divided brothers and sisters, it unites them and forms them into a family. . . .

Tomorrow everyone will be reunited. Through what means? First of all through the charity that establishes Jesus in our midst. With Jesus in our midst . . . we will reach the crown and summit . . . which is the eucharist.[57]

Jesus in our midst gives the light to resolve theological differences

Let's consider first of all the necessity Chiara feels that experiences of life should precede study. Speaking to a group of Evangelicals at Nuremberg, Germany in 1964, she tells of her impression "that Jesus in our midst is an ecumenical necessity." She continues explaining how, through the centuries, the one Church founded by Jesus divided itself and how today the Holy Spirit, through various means, has been working for years to restore unity, for example, through "ecumenical activities, the Council, and meetings among theologians." She concludes:

But I think that it would be very useful to allow life experience to precede study. And who is life? We know who it is: it is Jesus, Jesus in our midst. . . . In this ecumenical era, he can be both the way to unity and the life of unity that already exists, and it is he who will make the truth of the one Church of Christ shine forth.[58]

In all her ecumenical discourses Chiara points to the idea that Jesus in our midst is not only charity, but he is also the truth. Speaking of the existing relationship with the Evangelicals she says:

Together, we want to have Jesus in our midst, since our baptism makes this possible. Of one thing we are certain: Jesus is *the* theologian. And in our midst he is not only love, he is also truth. If we try to live in such a way that he be always in our midst, first seeking perhaps, as Pope John said, those things which unite us, little by little Jesus among us will give us a clear vision of the truth and will work out those theological differences which still separate us.[59]

In fact, truth is one ("it will have many aspects but it is still only one because it is Christ"), and Jesus in our midst brings everyone to freely accept it. To a group from the Reformed Church she explained:

Now if we go forward in reciprocal love, establishing an ever greater presence of Christ in our midst, with ever-deepened knowledge, which is the fruit of love . . . with patience, we will in time reach that moment in which Jesus in our midst will manifest his single truth, the single truth that we will freely accept. We will be united not only in charity, but also in unity of faith.[60]

Chiara does not overlook the theological difficulties, but affirms that Jesus in our midst creates the atmosphere in which they can be resolved.

He, because he is charity, makes our hearts exalt for our newfound brotherhood, paving the way for mutual understanding and knocking down centuries-old prejudices. But also, because he is the truth, he creates among Christian brothers and sisters, separated but united in him, that particular atmosphere that carries the breath of wisdom, that essential light for helping to resolve the various theological difficulties.[61]

"There are differences," she says elsewhere, "but they could disappear if theologians loved one another and placed Jesus in their midst."[62] It's marvelous to see how she explains—in an informal but significant way—the following "method" to a group from the Reformed Church and the Catholic Church gathered together.

It is surprising to see in ecumenical endeavors that while there is much recourse to study itself, there is little recourse to the Teacher. It would be necessary that all theologians, with the grace of God, become like children again, that they take the words of the gospel for what they are, and say: "Well, let's go to him, and there is only one of him. We are many Churches, but there is only one Jesus. Let's put him in our midst through our love for one another and let him enlighten us." Then one will say: "Ah, now I understand better what you are saying. I can follow your train of thought from this point to that one, but there is still something I do not understand." "Well then, let me try to explain it a bit further . . . this is what I mean." The other *becoming empty*, listens well, and with the light that comes from within says: "Ah, I think you're right. I'll hold onto that idea." Likewise the other, "Ah, I understand what you are saying now, let's keep that in mind." . . . It would really be something![63]

Jesus in our midst: an ecumenical hope

On various occasions when speaking to ecumenical groups, Chiara presented this concept:

Since what is humanly impossible is possible to God, if we, in our various denominations, have God in our midst, all things will be possible. Yes, because in the depths of our hearts we feel that, as an Anglican bishop said one Easter at a meeting of the Focolare in Rome, the more we come to know one another, the more the division becomes intolerable.[64]

Chiara, in fact, sees an ecumenical dimension in the entire charism of this spirituality. To a group of Anglicans, she said:

The charism of unity is one, and everyone can live it. . . .

The charism came to a Christian woman whom God had wished to be Catholic. In my opinion, however, it is not only for Catholics. It wouldn't make any sense. It is for all of Christianity. Therefore, it is not mine, it is not of the Catholic Church; it belongs to the mystical body of Christ.

What is its purpose? That of animating or giving a soul to all Christians. Other charisms will have the task of giving a body suitable to the soul. But it is our task to create the soul. This is of such importance, that it is the only thing that remains in heaven. As I was saying before, a Catholic and an Anglican who possess this charism and who truly live its spirit, have more of the kingdom of God among them than two Catholics (who do not love one another).[65]

Lastly, we note how not only Jesus in the midst of members of different Churches, but also Jesus in the midst in each single Church will bring to closer fulfillment the reality of the one Church of Christ. In this regard, the following is Chiara's explanation to a question addressed to her by an Evangelical youth.

Certainly, in God's plan various means have been put into motion to bring about the oneness of the Church of Christ. A line of action that I see very clearly is this: to increase the unity among Christians within the bounds of their respective Churches. This unity will make each Christian "more Jesus" and thus establish, though in different ways and degrees of intensity, the presence of Jesus in the midst in each Church. It will be Jesus in our midst who will highlight the already existing truths of each Church, but he will also point out the defects and the shortcomings in each Church. He will shed light on the beauty and the truth found in the mother Church and in the other Churches, and so facilitate a growth in communion until all will be one.[66]

From this very significant aspect, we'll pass on to the other dimension mentioned in this chapter's title, the social one.

Jesus, the perfect man

Where Jesus is truly present, we have the potential solution to every human problem, because he is humanity completely fulfilled. Such charismatic faith as this brings Chiara to state already in 1948, "And Jesus, *having become the bond* of Christians, will, in charity and truth, resolve every social problem."[67] Speaking about the beginning of the Focolare she states further, "One thing, however, is certain: the one who lived in our midst was God; we had with us the one who could answer all the questions that people could propose to him from every age and time."[68] Elsewhere she writes that "Jesus is the perfect man who contains within himself all of the human race and all truths," and therefore, "the person who has found this man has found the solution to every problem, human and divine."[69]

Not only is Jesus the perfect man, but because he is God, he is also omnipotent. In meditating on the possibility of having him among us, Chiara writes:

In this brotherhood, everywhere and with everyone, we need not anxiously try to sort out human problems on our own. If we so wish (and it is enough to be united in his name; that is, in him and in the way he wills it), Christ is among us and with us, he, the Almighty! This gives us hope. Yes, it gives us great hope.[70]

He is the only one capable of creating a truly new world, of transforming society. Writing to a group of the Focolare Chiara says:

The world needs to be enlightened, healed, and cleansed by a solid block of Christians among whom lives Christ, the only one capable of creating a *new world. This* is what we want.[71]

She earnestly advises, therefore, "Let's remain as we are, *united*. Then Jesus will work miracles and society little by little will change."[72]

With Jesus in our midst, a new social model can be offered. "By building the Work of Mary," Chiara says, "we are building a society in which others will see and witness that social problems are truly being solved."[73]

Furthermore, the life of Jesus in our midst is seen as the foundation for every Christian society.

> The norm of all norms, the premise of every other rule in every Christian society is the presence of Christ promised to the collectivity. "Where two or three are gathered together in my name, there am I in the midst of them."[74]

This norm can then extend itself to society in general. In fact, Chiara writes, "We want Christ to triumph in our midst so that one day he might be the single and most genuine expression of our society."[75]

Little Churches, local action cells

This human-social dimension, however, is also intrinsically linked with the ecclesial dimension. In fact, the true Church is the highest point of God's plan for humanity, and Jesus in our midst, as we have seen, is the "health" of this Church, the life of the Church carried into the smallest channels of human interaction. In the following text, after having spoken about the mutual love that establishes the presence of Jesus in the midst among two persons, Chiara describes this extensive network.

> We make ourselves one to the point of guaranteeing Jesus' presence, inasmuch as we can, and to the point of always advancing ahead like a little Church on its journey.

A Church even when we are at home, at school, at the office, or in legislature. Thus we walk along in life like the disciples of Emmaus with that third person among us, who gives divine value to all our activity.[76]

Elsewhere, Chiara gives a name to these small groups or "little Churches." She calls them "local action cells," "which are like little fires that are enkindled where Christ is in the midst of laborers, clerical workers, government officials, etc."[77]

These "cells" are none other than "living cells" of the Church which contribute to animating the society around them. Speaking of the presence of Jesus in our midst, which can be kept at all times, Chiara continues:

> If we do this, there will be an upsurge of vibrant cells in the Church which, in time, will be able to animate the society that surrounds them until the whole mass is penetrated. This mass, then, informed by the spirit of Christ, will be better able to fulfill God's plan for the world, and give a decisive thrust to a peaceful, irresistible social revolution bearing consequences we never dared hope for.

> If the historical Christ healed and satisfied the hunger of souls and bodies, Christ mystically present among his followers today knows how to do just the same. If the historical Christ asked his Father, before dying, for oneness among his disciples, Christ mystically present among Christians knows how to bring this about.[78]

For the very reason that "two or more" are enough no one can obstruct this presence of the Church; it can penetrate everywhere.

> It is a reciprocal love that can—even where the Church may be obstructed in its ministry—make Christ present among people's lives. Spiritually present, that is, but present nonetheless.[79]

Elsewhere she explains:

> Remember, there is no one who lacks what is necessary to offer Jesus to today's society. It is not necessary to have the freedom of the press; sermons and talks are not essential;

church buildings are not indispensable. When God takes everything away, there is nothing that is necessary.

There is a presence of Jesus that is possible to establish in every country, in every environment. It is a presence that has come to the forefront in our day and age, through the Second Vatican Council and also through our movement. It is the one which God offers us where there are two or more united in the name of Christ, whether they be in America, in Africa, or in Russia.[80]

In conclusion, therefore, the gift of Jesus in our midst is not an end in itself destined to remain within the bounds of a small closed group, but rather it is to be a wellspring for many, above all for those most in need.

In today's dechristianized and materialistic society, Christians, wherever they are, must build among themselves a spiritual cloister. If they themselves would be the columns, living water would flow in their midst for the use of many.[81]

"People who are healthy do not need a doctor; sick people do. . . . It is mercy I desire and not sacrifice. I have come to call not the self-righteous, but sinners" (Mt 9:12–13). This is the vocation of the historical Jesus.

It is the mission of *Jesus in the midst* of us.[82]

Jesus in our midst as the answer to the social and psychological needs of our times

In listing some of the needs of our times Chiara includes: group involvement, the sense of participation, and dialogue . . . and she explains how "all this is contained in the Christian ideal, and even more":

If we have Christ among us we can be the most exemplary *group* because we are cells of his Body, the Church.

We can live the fullest *participation* because unity does not exist without a complete love for all, without a giving of our entire selves.

99

We are able to initiate a constructive *dialogue*, modelled in some way on the life of the Holy Trinity, where the Divine Persons are eternally one and in loving dialogue.[83]

Speaking further on the modern aspirations for both autonomy and teamwork, etc., she observes that both needs are satisfied with Jesus in our midst. "What everyone aspires to, namely this new way of governing as is sought in universities and in political spheres, etc., we have already put into practice." She continues by explaining how in the Work of Mary there is "the perfect democracy in the equality of the children of God" and "the most decisive unity where all authority comes from above." She concludes, "We are both realities: we are freedom and unity in the highest sense of the words, for our life is a reflection on earth of the life of the Holy Trinity."[84]

The renewal of all the expressions of human life

In speaking of the effects the presence of Jesus in our midst produces, Chiara lists also, "the clarification of all human realities," wherein she refers to a renewal "in the fields of philosophy, politics, art, science, education, and all the expressions of human life."[85] The intuition of this dimension was already present in the early years. Describing that period Chiara says:

We understood that a new art would be born, a new education, a new medicine. . . . The Lord enlightened us on what little by little would be a concrete result of the Focolare's spirit: the presence of Jesus among artists, teachers, and doctors.[86]

In 1958 she spoke of "a closely bound international network of people grouped by categories (for example, philosophers, politicians, doctors, laborers, etc.)." She explained:

All the medical doctors of the Focolare, for example, would form a category of persons who, in the fire of the fraternal charity that must thrive among them as their first and irreplaceable law, would put into common their experiences in order to enhance the development of a Christian medicine emphasizing its collective dimension.

In each of the specific categories, the attempt is made—on the strength of the spirit that animates the Focolare—to resolve problems in a collegial manner. This intends to knock down the barriers formed between men and women workers, and those barriers formed by egoism that seeks first the advancement of one's personal career or finds only individual expression in living out professional, artistic, or scientific endeavors.

As within each category, there must also be perfect unity among the different categories, and this is to be achieved in a deeply Marian spirit, which loses the ego in the life of the community, and where the personality of each member, through charity, finds greater empowerment in God. It is Jesus who, through the Focolare, desires to reign amongst doctors, artists, and in all the various social categories.[87]

We will not enter any further into these particular aspects that Chiara mentions: education, politics, theological and psychological studies, art, and so on.

Rather, we will research the concrete methodologies that are followed in these fields of human endeavor, i.e., how do we go about preparing a lesson, or a talk, or painting a picture, all things that require the creativity of the individual, with Jesus in our midst? Intuition can lead us to an answer found in the following selection in which Chiara explains how she herself develops the text for a talk she is to present. On one hand, there is the individual work that must be done, but when this is completed, the second step is to review the work together with others so that it can be refined by Jesus in our midst.

It is said that St. Emyard, in preparing his sermon, had the habit of placing himself at his kneeler in a state of adoration. "There" he would say in his familiar manner, "I make the dough and set it to cook in the eucharistic oven."

Jesus in the eucharist was his spirituality.

Ours is Jesus in our midst.

For this reason, if we want to bear fruit when we speak, we must prepare ourselves well in deep meditation with Jesus inside of us and lay out the points of the talk.

But this is not enough. So that this "dough" might become bread that can be digested by those who listen, we must set it to cook over the flame of Jesus in the midst of a few of us.

Jesus in our midst corrects our outline. He advises us on what is superfluous or unnecessary. He enlightens us on what needs to be added, and above all he instructs us on the order in which the points should be organized, thus giving the talk that divine logic which allows the flow of thoughts to be delivered in "that" particular manner so as to produce for others the effects desired.[88]

Jesus in our midst knocks down divisions among social classes

We have seen above that the words "where two or more" leave it anonymous; meaning, they can be lived by everyone.[89] When they are lived, barriers and divisions fall. All involved look toward forming a universal society.

"Where two or more . . ." In putting these words into practice, we have seen barriers crumble on all sides. One such barrier has been the narrow-minded, fault-finding, and even hateful attitude often existing between persons of different neighborhoods, towns, or regions. Jesus among us overcame these examples of foolish human weakness when, for instance, someone from the city of Trent and someone from the neighboring town of Rovereto were united in his name.

Where there were two or more from different countries, the barrier of nationalism crumbled.

Where there were two or more from different racial backgrounds, racism crumbled.

Two or more—whoever they were, even when they had always been considered incompatible for reasons of culture, class, age, or whatever. . . . All could be, and indeed were meant to be, united in the name of Christ.[90]

And she continues:

The practice of living according to these words gave our community and our gatherings something of the atmosphere of the early Christian communities, helping to show the world that the Church is everyone's mother and a shining example of unity.[91]

Jesus in our midst and world order

We conclude this section with a few reflections on what significance this life would have if it were applied on a world-wide scale.

To begin with, living with Jesus in our midst is in itself a contribution toward peace. When praying for world peace one day in 1965, Chiara said, "But I understood that peace is Jesus himself. . . . Therefore, there is no better way to pursue true peace than in bringing Jesus into the world."[92]

On a prophetic note she speaks of the unity of all peoples, Jesus in the midst of nations. In referring to "that reciprocal love among nations that God asks for, as he asks for reciprocal love among brothers and sisters," Chiara affirms that, "if one day men and women, not as individuals, but as peoples . . . would learn how to put their own selves aside, including the idea they have of their own countries," out of love. "That day will mark the beginning of a new era, because on that day, just as there is the living presence of Jesus among two persons who love one another in Christ, there will be the living presence of Jesus among entire peoples. He will finally be given his rightful place as the one king, not only of people's hearts, but of nations."[93]

Describing the effects of love among nations, Chiara speaks of "a new phenomenon."

> Love discovers others to be similar to oneself or makes others similar. The peoples of the world will learn from the best qualities of one another. The different virtues will circulate among all and enrich all.
>
> Then there will truly be unity and diversity. A people will rise up in the world, and though child of the earth, will be clothed in the heavenly law, and will be able to call itself "the people of God."[94]

Concretely speaking, how do we reach such a unity among nations? Chiara indicates two roads. The first is to reach an ever greater fulfillment of this life among individuals.

> When . . . the life of the mystical body will be so developed among individuals, who *will love* their neighbors in an effective manner, whether white or black, red or yellow, *as themselves*, it will be easy to extend this law to reign among nations.[95]

She also speaks of diplomacy and how Jesus in the midst should be its animator.

> On a personal scale, if the actions of every diplomat were to be motivated by charity toward the other country as toward the country represented, God's help would greatly enlighten each one to make a contribution to establishing relationships among nations as they should be among individual persons . . . so that from heaven the Lord might see this new spectacle—his testament accomplished among the peoples of the earth.[96]

Chapter 4

JESUS IN OUR MIDST AND THE WORK OF MARY

If it is true, as we have ascertained, that the presence of Jesus in our midst has universal application, that its underlying charism is intended as a gift for the entire Church, and consequently, for all of humanity, it is also true that in order to present this gift, God focused his attention on a particular "religious family," a little society, a specific work in the Church, as he has almost always done in distributing his charisms throughout the centuries. The Work born from Chiara, as we have seen, is the Focolare movement, whose official name is the "Work of Mary."

In this chapter we will examine the role attributed to Jesus in our midst in the birth and development of the Work of Mary, in its governing capacity, in its various branches and concrete expressions, in the rule that defines its order, and lastly, as its name indicates, in its essentially Marian nature.

A. JESUS IN OUR MIDST: FOUNDER, LEGISLATOR, GUIDE AND SOUL OF THE WORK OF MARY

In describing the relationship of the presence of Jesus in our midst with the Work of Mary, Chiara underlines its fundamental role: "For us, since the beginning, Jesus in our midst was everything. He was life."[1] Elsewhere she specifies: "He is the founder, the sustainer, the maker, the builder . . . he is everything. It is Jesus who sustains everything. He is the soul of everything."[2]

Let's take a closer look at some of these qualities.

Jesus in our midst: the founder

In her book *May They All Be One,* Chiara describes the effects of the presence of Jesus in our midst.

> If we were asked what else the presence of Jesus in our midst means to the Focolare, we would have to answer that he has been its *founder* and its *legislator*; in the sense that the Focolare now has a certain structure which has been approved by the Church; and this structure is simply the result of our efforts, day by day, to discern the various ideas that we felt Jesus in our midst was suggesting to us as we tried to live in unity with one another and with the hierarchy.[3]

But the significance of the affirmation, often repeated by Chiara, that Jesus in our midst is the founder of the Focolare can be traced back even before the various structures were formed. It goes back to the Focolare's "conception," where it joins the very first ideas that animated the small initial group. "He gave rise to what we today call the Work of Mary."[4]

While stating this, Chiara does not deny her personal role in being a particular instrument of God. During an informal gathering she was asked, "Who is the founder of the Work of Mary?" Her reply: "We would have to take a close look, because Jesus also uses his instruments. But if you look at the instrument, you will soon come to know who it is." She continues by drawing immediate attention to Jesus in our midst. She sees how God had prepared various means, not only one. He prepared her, and gave her the original idea. However, he also prepared those who could become empty of themselves; that is, persons "capable of understanding this idea in such a way that from the very first instant this spirituality came to light, it came to light as Jesus in our midst." She concludes: "What did Jesus in our midst do? He enlightened us and we went forward to found the Work of Mary. Who founded it? Jesus in our midst."[5]

Jesus in our midst: the legislator

This concept is closely linked to Jesus in our midst the founder. We will consider Jesus in our midst as legislator in the specific sense that it was he who suggested the principal ideas that were later assumed into the Statutes of the Work of Mary. Chiara explains:

> The Work of Mary is a majestic work in the Church, for which God had drawn very precise lines. But who suggested them to us? They didn't come from our human intellect, nor our reasoning. It was Jesus in our midst who assisted us, who made us aware of what God wanted of us; he designed a path that was meant not only for us, but for everyone.[6]

The various vocations of the Work of Mary were also born from Jesus in the midst, as were their norms of life.

> And who, then, throughout the entire history of the Focolare, traced those lines of light for its organization?
>
> Who else could have given birth to the various vocations but he? Each vocation is divine and so, too, is each application of the same Ideal lived in the various callings.
>
> He is the one behind our norms of life, behind every step we take.[7]

Also here, Chiara does not deny her personal role. "We had always put Jesus in our midst," she explains. "Consequently, I would understand, for example, the order our lifestyle should take, and what norms we should give to our life. These ideas were then presented to the Church, who accepted them as our Rule."[8] Chiara calls to mind, however, that "notwithstanding the talents which some of us in the Work of Mary may have had, it has always and without doubt been Jesus in our midst in the Focolare that gave origin to and developed every particular aspect."[9]

Jesus in our midst: the sustainer, guide, and soul

Here is a further affirmation on the role of Jesus in our midst in the Work of Mary.

He is its sustainer.

> He is the sustainer of the Focolare. His presence, even in the most painful and difficult moments, has practically always been our one comfort.[10]

Jesus in our midst is also guide and leader. "We went forward" says Chiara, "spurred on by Jesus in our midst. Our superior, leader and guide was always Jesus in our midst."[11] This is true in a particular way because he alone knows the future of the Work of Mary, the plan God has for it.

> Jesus in our midst is our *commander in chief* in the battles which the Focolare is called to wage on all fronts: those where lines have already been established and need to be held and fortified; and other positions, at first unfamiliar, where Jesus sends us from time to time. For God alone knows his complete plan for the Focolare, and Jesus in our midst reveals it to us a little at a time.[12]

Lastly, Jesus in our midst is the soul of the Work of Mary. Chiara, in fact, affirms it explicitly. "If you ask me what place Jesus in our midst holds in the Work of Mary, I would answer that he is its soul."[13] Chiara compares him to "His Majesty" in St. Teresa of Avila's *Interior Castle.*

> [The Work of Mary] is like an exterior castle opened up in the midst of the Church, a castle all-illuminated. . . .
>
> And what is the light of this Work of Mary? It is Jesus in our midst. . . .
>
> Jesus is "His Majesty" of the kingdom of Mary, of this castle of the kingdom of Mary.[14]

We have seen that the principal ideas of the Work of Mary, its structure and its life were born from Jesus in our midst. The moment came when the Church requested that this way of life be formulated in writing, as a rule that the Church herself was to approve and establish as the Focolare's norm of life.

The history of the various drafts of this rule is an interesting one, but would demand a lengthy study of its own. Let's just say, for clarification, that seven successive drafts were made (each one assisted by an expert of canon law appointed by the Church). Is was only the last draft that received a definitive approval, the one also that Chiara herself felt truly corresponded to what came to birth through Jesus in their midst.[15]

For this reason Chiara was able to say:

We can hold that the masterpiece of Jesus in our midst is precisely this rule.

It is a rule that he carefully shaped day by day, hour by hour, inspiration by inspiration. There is a wonderful fusion between what God over time has revealed to us, and what God suggests to the Church, who has governed souls throughout the centuries.[16]

Lastly, we want to also consider the role that Jesus in our midst played in composing the text of the rule. In describing the work entailed, Chiara recalls: "we had only one concern—to have Jesus in our midst."[17]

Jesus in the midst as expressed in the various rules

Besides his being present in putting the rule together, Jesus in the midst is also present in its contents. We will trace a few historical developments.

In the first outline of the statutes compiled for diocesan approval (granted on May 1, 1947, for one year and renewed the following year for another three years) there is no specific mention of "Jesus in our midst." One statement does read, however:

> The Association intends, through example and through works, to promote in the midst of the world the central idea of the gospel: charity, under the form of its most perfect expression: unity, understood as the fulfillment of Jesus' will and testament, "may they all be one" (Jn 17:21).[18]

The 1951 draft of the statutes, which we amply cited in a previous section,[19] treated at length the topic of unity. It then described the life of the focolare center.

> We are looking therefore at a home. A home where many true members of a family live with Jesus in their midst, with the Father, and with Mary.
>
> The focolare center is essentially a church, a temple, the temple of the living God. Not because of any external images (which should be there, as in a normal family), but because of a continuous, warm, silent, constructive, fruitful, luminous presence of God among souls united in the name of Jesus.
>
> In all the focolare centers, Jesus must live in and among their members, through whom and in whom the Father of all these children becomes present.
>
> Therefore, besides being Jesus' home, it is also Mary's because it is the home of her children. That particular atmosphere indicative of Mary's presence must be felt. Just as the breath of the Holy Spirit moved about among the first Christian communities, whose members were of one heart and one soul, so too in the focolare centers where unity must reign, the breath of the Holy Spirit, Mary's spouse, must freely move about.[20]

We notice that the style of the draft is not heavily juridical,[21] and we also take note of the various references linking Jesus in our midst with the three persons of the Trinity. This same article, transcribed into the 1954 draft, becomes even more specific in its mention of Jesus in our midst when citing the verse of Matthew 18:20.

We are looking therefore at a home. A home where many true members of a family live with Jesus in their midst. ". . . For where two or more are gathered together in my name, there am I in the midst of them" (Mt 18:20).

In the focolare center, God must dwell in the midst of its members bound in charity.[22]

The document also states:

Born in the light of *Mystici Corporis* they will feel drawn to foster *among themselves* (so as to be extended to many and to everyone if possible) that *unity* for which Jesus implored the Father in his testament. They will not move about or engage in any activity that does not stem from such a unity wherein, together with that union with God attained through union with one another, they will encounter the death of their egos, the training grounds for their own sanctity.[23]

In the third draft of the statutes, composed at the request of Pius XII in 1958, there also appears an explicit mention of Jesus in our midst as the bond between the Focolare's members, formulated in the following terms:

The members of the Work of Mary, in coming to know and love one another constantly and concretely, are united in the name of Jesus, for which reason they hope and believe to have *Jesus in their midst* as he himself had promised: "Where two or more are gathered together in my name, there am I in the midst of them" (Mt 18:20).[24]

Finally, in the statutes which were granted approval in 1962, article nine contains a very clear affirmation that was also printed on its cover as an introduction to the entire booklet.

The Focolarini must work toward always meriting the fulfillment of Jesus' promise made to all who are united in his holy name: "Where two or more are gathered together in my name, there am I in the midst of them" (Mt 18:20). The mutual and constant charity, intended by Jesus and taught by

111

the Church, which renders possible the presence of Jesus in the collectivity, is for the Focolarini the principal concept which inspires their every activity, whether it concern their spiritual or their apostolic lives. For them it is the norm of all norms, the premise for all other rules, as called for by God and interpreted by the Church.[25]

At this point, Jesus in our midst is affirmed to be the basic characteristic of the Focolare.[26]

Jesus in our midst: the premise for every other rule

The fundamental importance given to Jesus in our midst, which even precedes the rule itself, had already been expressed in the statute's outline tracing back to 1950.

So that the Order of Mary might correspond to that purpose for which God formed it, it proposes the following as the first point of its statutes.

This statute holds valid only after the presence of *Jesus in the midst* has been established in the order or in the Focolare. The moment this is lacking, the superior has the obligation not to follow it, so as to first reestablish the presence of Jesus in their midst, given that: *porro unum est necessarium* (only one thing is required) . . .[27]

In the statutes approved in 1962, there appears the phrase "the premise for every other rule." Commenting on this Chiara explains: "This rule is valid provided there is first Jesus in our midst: then, one may give a command, or obey, vows may be taken, there may be an active apostolate—but, there must be Jesus in our midst." She concludes, "this safeguards everything."[28]

Years later, Chiara comments once again on this fundamental concept of Jesus in our midst as the "norm of norms."

A few days ago, I was struck by the fact that on the very first page of our rule we presented the phrase that regards

Jesus in our midst as the synthesis of our vocation, as the norm of every other norm. In fact, the rule holds its validity only *if* he is present.

How can we then think of a focolare center that exists for even just one minute without Jesus in its midst?

In such a situation the Focolarini would be like monks without their habits, without their monastery, without their rule, without their daily schedule and without their superior, etc.

All that the Focolarini accomplish outside of his presence is wasted, has no value, falls into nothingness, has no access to heaven, and does not cause us to progress, in fact, just the opposite!

Jesus in our midst is everything for us.[29]

In recalling that this article of the statutes is followed by notes referring to the verses of Matthew 22:36–40, Mark 12:28–31 and John 13:24–35, Chiara notes how it is the Church herself that confirms and explains through the rule why Jesus in our midst is the "norm of norms."

It is the Church herself that says it. She says so confirming it with the gospel, which concludes that the entire law can be summarized in love for God and neighbor, and love for one another out of love for God. There are not greater commandments than these, in which the whole of the law and the Prophets are contained. This is the reason why we live a reciprocal charity that establishes Jesus in our midst; he is the norm of norms, the premise for every other rule, including the one we are presently speaking of.[30]

This is why his presence is always a must. In fact, Chiara states that "the kingdom of God *must* be in our midst, not *can* be, and when it is, we cannot sit back, because the kingdom must be there the moment that follows." And Chiara explains: "because—the Church says—Jesus in our midst is the premise of all other premises, he is the premise for the spiritual progress of souls as well as for their apostolate."[31] However, in contemplating the hypothetical case of a Focolarino found isolated from the others, Chiara recalls that the general purpose established in the rule is "the perfection of charity." She comments, "therefore, the perfection of Jesus in our midst is not always required of us, but what is always required is the perfection of charity."[32]

The rule safeguards Jesus in our midst

We'll conclude with this very brief mention of a concept that is opposite and complementary to the preceding one (Jesus in our midst: the premise of every other rule). This concept is that "the rule itself safeguards Jesus in our midst."[33] Chiara intends this to mean that the charism which she has received has been locked into the rule. Therefore, in conforming to the rule, the members can carry out the essence of the charism.[34]

C. JESUS IN OUR MIDST WITHIN THE VARIOUS BRANCHES AND EXPRESSIONS OF THE WORK OF MARY

What we have presented in terms of the rule holds valid first of all for the consecrated members of the Focolare, but it expresses a disposition that underlies the life of the entire movement in all its expressions and in each of its sections and branches.[35]

In fact, Chiara sees the witness of Jesus in our midst as the vocation of the Work of Mary as a whole, the reason for which it came to exist. "Since today the world seems to want to do without God, there needed to be a movement that could say: 'God exists . . . come, you'll find him in our midst.'"[36]

Jesus in our midst is what above all characterizes the focolare center and the life of the Focolarini. This is why Chiara compares the focolare center to the house of Nazareth.

> The focolare center is a home which houses members of the mystical body who, united in charity, have Jesus mystically present in their midst.

The focolare center must resemble the house of Nazareth, where Jesus was physically present among Mary and Joseph.[37]

"Without Jesus among its members," Chiara writes elsewhere, "the focolare center no longer exists."[38]

In her book, *Jesus in Our Midst*, Chiara defines the focolare center as "a small community which has Jesus in its midst."[39] In comparing this form of life to monastic life she observes: "When God thought of founding monasteries, for example, his idea then was the same."[40] However, even though she finds various passages in the writings of the Church Fathers, above all in the rule of St. Basil, which indicate how the primitive monastic life knew and lived this presence of Jesus, Chiara illustrates the originality of the focolare center, with its particular rule that orders life according to specific aspects, "aspects that change the outer appearance of and facilitate in their turn the presence of Jesus in our midst."[41]

Also the families that have Jesus in their midst can, in a certain sense, be called focolare centers. In speaking about families where both husband and wife live this spirit in a total way, Chiara says: "What will occur is a multiplication of the focolare centers in the world, because wherever there is Jesus in the midst there is a focolare center." And then she adds, "it is not because we are consecrated that [the places where] we [live] are focolare centers, but because there is Jesus in our midst."[42]

Jesus in our midst is what characterizes the temporary and permanent Mariapolises. At the closing of a summer meeting in 1960, Chiara exclaimed: "Jesus in our midst. This is what a Mariapolis is!"[43]

On one occasion, when speaking about the permanent Mariapolis of Loppiano, in Italy, Chiara stated that Jesus in its midst is its specific vocation, which makes it an anticipation of the new Jerusalem.

[The Mariapolis] teaches you the way to have Christ continually resurrect *among all of you*. Christ alive in your midst.

This, I would say, is the *specific* vocation of the Mariapolis, the purpose for which God brought this little city to life,

115

an anticipation of the heavenly Jerusalem of which it is written: "I saw the holy city, and the new Jerusalem, coming down from God out of heaven, as beautiful as a bride all dressed for her husband. Then I heard a loud voice call from the throne, 'You see this city? Here God lives among its people. He will make his home among them; they shall be his people and he will be their God . . .'" (Rv 21:2–4).

God, Jesus, spiritually alive in your midst, must never be lacking *here.*

If he is not here, if his presence fades, the vocation of the Mariapolis will be endangered.[44]

Elsewhere, in underlining the witness that the Mariapolis gives through the presence of Jesus in its midst, Chiara says that "it is this presence of Jesus, whose Spirit can be detected in the homes, the work places, the schools, and in the interpersonal relationships that makes Loppiano, even in the midst of its inevitable human weaknesses, a city on the mountain top which all can see."[45]

Such holds true for the other forms of life in the Focolare. Chiara explains:

What we have said here about the focolare centers holds as well for those other forms of living in unity present in the Focolare. We might call them temporary focolare units, such as the nuclei of Volunteers, of priests, of men and women religious, the Gen units, and so on, provided that they too remain all day long in unity of spirit with the other members of the nucleus, the unit, and the other members of the entire Work of Mary, so as to always have the presence of Jesus in their midst.[46]

Therefore, what Chiara says to the Gen in speaking of the various sources of God (the eucharist, the hierarchy of the Church, the gospel, etc.) is also valid for the entire movement. She underlines for all the members of the Focolare the fundamental importance of Jesus in our midst: "for us . . . all these different sources must work together in helping us to above all allow God to triumph in our midst."[47]

D. JESUS IN OUR MIDST, THE ONE WHO GOVERNS THE WORK OF MARY

We have seen how Chiara considers Jesus in our midst as the founder, legislator, and guide of the Work of Mary. And this, not only at one time in the past, but continually. He is the one who still today governs the Work of Mary. He is the superior. We'll take a look at several affirmations of this function of his in general, and a few more detailed descriptions on how this is lived in the focolare center.

Jesus in our midst, the true superior of each community

In formulating the text of the rule in 1960, Chiara observed that there existed certain terms which she felt were inappropriate, for example, the term *capo* (head), "because we feel that the head of the Work of Mary is Jesus in our midst."[48] She wrote:

Jesus in our midst is also the true *superior* of every focolare center. Because of the love that circulates among the members, he enlightens those charged with guiding the others. He does this also because those in positions of responsibility have a special grace to teach others, first and foremost, that their top priority must always be to have Jesus present in their midst.[49]

Chiara continues:

When a focolare center, or a branch, or region of the Focolare is set up according to the guidelines that God has given us and which the Church has approved, then in some way God speaks through those in authority. For in this movement which he has raised up, nourished, molded and structured, those in authority have but one task: to interpret his wishes.[50]

In the "zones" of the Work of Mary, that is, the various geographical sectors into which it is divided so as to give order to its life, another aspect of this "single authority" of Jesus in our midst is rendered visible. When the various sections collaborate in common activities, the representatives responsible for both the men's and women's sections have equal juridical standing.

> There is not just one single authority figure for the zone. The two juridical entities strive to be united in the name of Christ, so that when working in common, they have Jesus in their midst.

> Therefore the overall head is truly and only Jesus, who accomplishes his work by revealing himself through the unity established among people's lives.[51]

This happens also, though in a different way, for the general council of the Work of Mary, where the president and the co-president, though having different functions, must have Jesus in their midst. Looking toward the future, Chiara says: "at the moment of my death, I would in no way want to leave the Work of Mary in the hands of one person alone, but rather to Jesus in the midst of two persons. If there has been a charism at work . . . it has been precisely that of 'where two or more are gathered together in my name,' that is, the idea of Jesus in our midst."[52]

How the relationship of authority is lived in the focolare center

We mentioned above that the rule calls for superiors. In the specific case of the Focolarini, there involves also a vow of obedience. How is the relationship of obedience lived in the focolare center, and how is it linked with Jesus in its midst? Chiara describes a dual relationship.

> There is a dual relationship in the focolare center: one of equality and one hierarchical. The Focolarini are all equal because they are all members of the mystical body of Christ. No one is father because there is only one father for all the members of the mystical body, the one who is in heaven.

118

All are brothers and sisters, yet among them there lives the first-born brother who is Jesus in their midst. He is the true and single authority in the focolare center.

In concrete terms, since the focolare center functions as a little society, and in consideration of what St. Paul says that we are all members one of the other (cf. Rom 12:4–5), there is in the focolare center one who functions as the center of unity and represents Jesus among all. Besides love, he or she is also owed obedience, but it is an obedience lived in love. Doing the will of this person is doing God's will.[53]

Obedience lived in reciprocal charity is an enlightened obedience. Chiara explains:

There are superiors and there are those subject to them, but because of the love existing among them (because there is Jesus in their midst) all appear as brothers or sisters in the manner in which the gospel demands. It reads: *"Omnes vos fratres estis," "Nolite vocare . . ."*

If there is charity and if obedience is lived in perfect charity which demands the complete denial of self, the death of our ego in other terms, God comes to live among the united group for there is obedience among subordinates and superiors.

We established the idea that obedience lived in this way is never blind; it is enlightened. In fact, if Jesus is present among superiors and subordinates, Jesus is also present in one and in the other. This results that in the superior there is not just a human person who commands, but Jesus in that person. In regard to the subordinate, it is not just the human person who obeys, it is Jesus in that person who obeys.[54]

The following is a description of the practical method involved in reaching this enlightened obedience.

The superior, with detachment (and therefore as a gift of love) expresses what the subordinate must do. . . .

The subordinate, with detachment, expresses the personal difficulties that come into play which may indicate that God's will is another.

The superior then, as a communal gift, interprets the desire of Jesus in their midst which will result not only as to the liking of the subordinate (to his or her new self), but also as the only road to take.[55]

All "offer" their ideas out of love. Chiara, in fact, explains that putting aside one's ideas "does not mean to renounce them, but to offer them in order to arrive at the exact idea called for. This idea then becomes ours, or must be made ours with all the heart, soul, and spirit necessary to put it into practice."[56] Furthermore, to offer one's ideas is an obligation.

It is not that we *can* try to make ourselves better understood in relation to the responsible of the focolare center, but rather we *must* make ourselves better understood to the responsible of the focolare center. Why, at times, are we so timid and fearful! . . . We betray Jesus in our midst when we lack the courage to share our personal thoughts . . . provided they be expressed as gifts of love so that it is Christ, not my idea, that triumphs in our midst.[57]

This leads into a very original description of obedience.

Obedience is also a way of living God.

In fact, we do not go to our superiors in order to *have* a certain form of obedience in doing one thing or another. We go to them in order to offer, with detachment, our most genuine thought; therefore, to *give*, which means to love.

The superior then, in being loved responds with love and thus Jesus lives among the two.

The superior says what Jesus in their midst would say.

The subordinate knows that the superior's wish is the will of God (not of a human person) and therefore gladly obeys because one obeys what actually lies in the depth of the heart. In fact, in approaching the superior in a spirit of love, the subordinate has the Spirit of Jesus, who in the midst of the two speaks more clearly through the words of the superior.

The subordinate, therefore, obeys God in oneself, which is the best of oneself, becoming therefore free, God, Jesus.[58]

We began by speaking about the dual relationship between subordinates and their superiors being at once fraternal and involving obedience. In a further explanation Chiara uses two analogies. In the first she compares this dual relationship to the relationship that each member of the mystical body has with Jesus: "Jesus is the brother of every member, and loves each member to the point of death, death on the cross. At the same time, he is also the members' 'head.'"[59] In the second analogy Chiara considers the relationship between Jesus and the Father.

It is what happens between Jesus and the Father: in the relationship of Jesus with the Father, both aspects are superimposed.

Jesus loved the Father. He loved him so much as to become one with him.

He says of himself: "The one who sees me, sees the Father."

The Father was in him through love.

Obedience, in Jesus, is therefore an expression of love toward the Father. . . .

In the focolare center, charity is the basis for every relationship, and only on this level is the relationship of authority established. This was Jesus' disposition in regards to the Father.

Jesus' obedience to the Father, being an expression of love for the Father, was as profound as his love, in the sense that it carried the death of self, even death on the cross.

Therefore, for love of the Father he nullified his own way of thinking and wishing, his entire self.

The subordinate must act in a similar way toward the superior. . . .

The superior then, on his or her own account, in taking the place of the Father, gives one's entire self as an expression of love because the command itself must also be given in charity and through charity. . . .

In this kind of reciprocal love, there is truly present the relationship between Jesus and the Father.

In fact, among the subordinate and the superior there is Jesus in their midst; Jesus who makes them one.

What happens is that in the subordinate there is the superior, and in the superior, the subordinate, just as in Jesus there is the Father and in the Father, Jesus.[60]

In conclusion, the following statement can serve as a summary of what has been said thus far about this dual relationship in the focolare center. Chiara says:

The *porro unum* (one thing required) is love. In the focolare centers the first thing to build, without which the rest has no meaning, is love. . . . In this atmosphere of reciprocal love, obedience also finds its place.[61]

E. JESUS IN OUR MIDST AND MARY

We have seen that a cardinal point of Chiara's spirituality is the presence of Jesus in our midst and the important role it plays in the work she has founded. It is the premise, in fact, for everything else that follows. Nevertheless, the name given to this work, is the "Work of Mary."[62]

In this last section we will consider the relationship between Jesus in our midst and Mary, without entering, however, into the many other reasons that link this particular Work with Mary.

Mary and the birth of the Focolare

Chiara, in speaking about the birth of the Focolare, defines it as "a heavenly invention shaped by Mary's motherly care whose purpose is to form children similar to her."

A beautiful detail to note is that the first of Chiara's writings to specifically mention the concept of Jesus in our midst speaks also of Mary, as the one who wants us united.

It is our mother who makes us meet one another along the way of God's love.

We were already walking along that luminous way.

Our mother wants us united on our journey! She knows that "where two or more" unite in the holy name of her son, *he is in their midst. . . .*

It is Mary, who taking us by the hand unites us; she fuses us always more in unity to the point that we consume ourselves in unity![63]

If there was little mention of Mary in the early years, her role in nurturing unity however, was understood. Chiara had said:

Mary is the door which leads us to God. A door is not a door unless it is opened to allow someone to pass through. . . . Whoever stops at the door does not reach God. The door leads to Jesus.

Unity points toward the goal and contains in itself the means. The means disappears at the sight of the goal. But only the one who has truly reached the goal, blesses the means.[64]

Mary is seen therefore as the means to unity.

To live Mary

But let's turn back our attention to the specific relationship between Jesus in our midst and Mary.

Besides Mary being the one who wants us united, and who leads us to this way, there is another fundamental relationship involved. We, in generating—so to speak—Jesus in our midst, repeat in a collective way what Mary herself had done. "We live Mary." Chiara explains.

In order to establish the presence of Jesus in our midst we take on the role of Mary. . . . We generate Jesus in our midst by means of reciprocal love. Our role therefore is a marian one. To put Jesus in our midst requires a marian role, since it is a matter of generating Christ's presence.[65]

In this particular aspect Christians of other Churches also find their bearings. When speaking on one occasion to a group of Anglicans Chiara recounted her dialogue with the Evangelicals. She began by bringing everyone to recognize that, in concrete terms, what Mary had done was to give Jesus physically to the world and what the Focolare does is to give to the world his spiritual presence. She continued:

> You ... have a deep appreciation for this spirituality; remember: each time you gather into unity so as to have Jesus spiritually in your midst, you imitate Mary. Without realizing it, you are followers of Mary. And even if you do not consider her your mother, she still sees you as her children, because that is who you are.[66]

Commenting on the impression left upon the group of Evangelicals, Chiara concluded by saying: "they seemed very, very pleased."[67]

This fundamental rapport between Jesus in our midst and Mary leads the way into two other aspects of relationship with Mary. Mary is the model for the Focolare's life and activity, and the Work of Mary is, in a certain way, a mystical presence of Mary in the Church.

Mary: model for the Focolare

Mary is the Focolare's model because she expresses and contains in herself the life of the mystical body.

> In its essence, this life, apart from the particular forms that the Focolarini, as children of the Church, must assume, can otherwise be lived by all the religious, priests, laity, families, and by society itself because it is the life of the mystical body. It is a marian life, and everyone can find themselves in Mary.
>
> Mary is the type, the model member of the mystical body for in her all graces were brought to fruition and none was lost.

124

She is in some way the synthesis of the mystical body, a little church which stands before Jesus, the head of the Church.[68]

This links her in a specific way to Jesus in our midst.

Mary is the model of every member of the Focolare because, as hers was the primary role of being the mother of the physical Christ, the Focolare—as we have seen—has as its most essential role that of bringing into the world, in the words of a bishop—the spiritual presence of Christ among people today.[69]

A mystical presence of Mary

Behind this way of imitating Mary in giving Jesus to the world, there is an intuition of a mystical, ontological kind that Chiara received during that period of light and particular graces which we spoke about before. "We seemed to understand" she writes, "that the Work that was being born would have come to be nothing else than a mystical presence of Mary in the Church."[70]

Among Fr. Alberione's writings, Chiara found an analogous statement: "The Pauline family was brought to life by St. Paul in order to continue his work. It is St. Paul alive today but composed of many members." Chiara comments: "Don't we say that the Work of Mary was formed by Mary so as to be a continuation of her presence on earth today, and that it is . . . Mary alive, but composed today of many members?"[71]

Elsewhere, she links this concept with Jesus in our midst saying that the words "in our midst" give the idea that we surround him, that we are, so to speak, "his heaven." "So I say" Chiara comments, "wherever the Work of Mary is established, there is Christ in its midst, surrounded by Mary because the Work of Mary is the mystical presence of Mary and therefore the heaven of Jesus in our midst."[72]

The name of the Work of Mary

As we mentioned before, there are many reasons for linking the Focolare to the person of Mary, and many intuitions about her that will remain undeveloped in this particular study. But the greatest reason, perhaps, for this linkage is the relationship between Mary and Jesus in our midst. In this light the Work of Mary lives its marian role, furthermore it is a marian presence. This is the explanation for its name. In fact, Chiara herself poses the question as to why the name "Work of Mary." "Is it because we wanted to give a certain title to Mary or because we see in her a person who embraces everyone?" "No," she answers, and explains:

> It is because when Mary was on earth, her work was not to found a religious order or a convent. Her work was Jesus. The work of Mary that lives in the Work of Mary is Jesus in our midst. Therefore, Jesus in our midst makes us Mary, makes us the Work of Mary.[73]

We conclude this selection of passages from Chiara's writings with the following text of her diary that ties different points together, making a very beautiful synthesis.

> Jesus in our midst, I would say, is our great charism. The most simple and sublime things that arise among the lives of human beings come from above. It is the spiritual return of Christ among a group of his disciples, and therefore in the Church.
>
> It is not essential to speak or to write at length about it.
>
> What is important is to give *him* to the world as Mary did and to learn to do only that. All the rest will follow as a consequence.[74]

ABBREVIATIONS

In citing works in the notes, short titles have generally been used. Works frequently cited have been identified by the following abbreviations:

AAS   *Acta Apostolicae Sedis,* the Vatican gazette. Carries the original text of important Vatican documents.

F   Austin Flannery, O.P., *Vatican II: Councilar and Postcounciliar Documents* (New York: Costello Publishing Co., 1986). Volume 1 of "Vatican Collection."

LET   Letter of Chiara Lubich.

REC   Recording of Chiara Lubich.

Scr. Sp./1   Lubich, Chiara, *Scritti Spirituali/1. L'attrattiva del Tempo Moderno,* (Spiritual writings/1. The attraction of modern times) (Rome: Città Nuova, 1978). A collection of three titles: *Meditazioni* (Meditations), Rome, 1959; *Pensieri* (Thoughts), Rome, 1961; and *Frammenti* (Fragments), Rome, 1963.

Scr. Sp./2   Lubich, Chiara, *Scritti Spirituali/2. L'essenziale di oggi,* (Spiritual writings/2. What's essential today) (Rome: Città Nuova, 1978). A collection of two titles: *Saper Perdere* (Knowing how to lose), Rome, 1969; and *Sí, Sí, No, No* (Yes, yes, no, no) Rome, 1973.

Scr. Sp./3   Lubich, Chiara, *Scritti Spirituali/3. Tutti Uno,* (Spiritual writings/3. All one) (Rome: Città Nuova, 1979). A collection of four titles: *Tutti Siano Uno* (That all may be one), Rome, 1968; *La Carità Come Ideale* (Charity as an ideal), Rome, 1971; *Parola di Vita* (The Word of life), Rome, 1975; and *Dove Due o Tre . . .* (Where two or three . . .), Rome, 1976.

WRIT   Unpublished writing of Chiara Lubich.

NOTES

Preface

1. C. Lubich, *Unity and Jesus Forsaken* (New York: New City Press, 1985), 91.

2. J. Bacik, *Contemporary Theologians* (Chicago: The Thomas More Press, 1989), 43.

3. R. Burrows, *To Believe in Jesus* (Danville, NJ: Dimension Books, 1981), 53.

4. S. Fitzgerald, ed., *The Habit of Being: Letters of Flannery O'Connor* (New York: Farrar, Straus and Giroux, 1979), 453.

5. J. Shea, *Stories of God: An Unauthorized Biography* (Chicago: Thomas More Association, 1978), 152.

6. R. Siegfried and R. Morneau, eds., *Selected Poetry of Jessica Powers* (Kansas City, MO: Sheed and Ward, 1989), 152.

Introduction

1. Chiara Lubich was born in Trent, Italy in 1920 and is the current president of the Focolare movement. The Focolare began in 1943 and was granted its first diocesan approval by Bishop Carlo de Ferrari of Trent in 1947, while the initial pontifical approval was given by Pope John XXIII in 1962. For the Focolare movement's approval cf. M. Ingoldsby, "The Focolare Movement," in *L'Osservatore Romano—Weekly Edition in English*, X (March 7, 1974), 6-8. In 1977 Chiara Lubich was awarded the Templeton Prize for progress in religion, the news of which was printed in at least 764 newspapers of 34 nations.

2. Cf. *Paolo VI al Movimento dei Focolari*, (Rome, 1978).

3. Cf. E. Robertson, *Chiara* (Ireland, 1976).

4. Cf. C. Lubich, "Cristo nella comunità," in *Città Nuova*, XXII (1978), 40.

5. For a general view cf. "Where Two or Three," in C. Lubich, *May They all Be One* (New York: New City Press, 1984), 79-91 (hereafter *All One*).

6. *Dogmatic Constitution on Divine Revelation*, 8b, in F, 754.

7. G. Rossè, *Gesú in mezzo: Matteo 18, 20 nell' esegesi contemporanea*, (Rome: Città Nuova, 1972).

8. K. Hemmerle, *Die Himmel ist zwischen uns*, (Munich, 1977).

9. Cf. C. Lubich, "La mia testimonianza di vita e di fede" (a talk given by Chiara Lubich to the nineteenth National Eucharistic Congress, Pescara, Italy September 15, 1977), found in *Scr. Sp./1*, 9-23.

10. *Scr. Sp./1*, 13.

11. REC May 10, 1969 (Loppiano, Italy).

12. Cf. G. Lubich, "Cosí nacque il focolare," Interview of Chiara Lubich, in *Città Nuova*, XIX, 13 (1975), 34.

13. LET February 2, 1945 ("Carissime sorelline . . ."). While reading this letter during a prepared talk, REC December 7, 1971, (Rocca di Papa, Italy, to the focolarini), Chiara commented: "From what we can see . . . we were not yet living with Jesus in our midst."

14. Cf. *Scr. Sp. /1*, 11.

15. LET 1944-45 (?) ("Sorelle mie! . . .").

16. WRIT December 12, 1946. Notes prepared for a meeting of young people of the Third Order of St. Francis.

17. WRIT December 2, 1946. The word "combination" in this context is being used as an analogy of a chemical combination.

18. LET September 6, 1947 (Fiera di Primiero, Italy, "Carissima C. e compagne . . ."). Naturally, the understanding of Mt. 18:20 could have come earlier. Igino Giordani [see note 25] speaks of the life of Jesus in the midst of the first focolare center in the years 1944-45 (I. Giordani, "Storia del 'Movimento dei Focolari,'" unedited text for internal use, Rocca di Papa, Italy 1977, V. I, 53-54). And in a letter of February 27, 1948, ("Padre B . . ."), Chiara speaks of Jesus "who we have been bringing *among us* for years" and also says, "Jesus is among them and he will tell them everything he has told us during our life of unity over these years." But, in either case we cannot establish whether it is a question of experience alone or its linkage already to Mt. 18:20.

19. C. d. T., "Questa è l'ora di S. Francesco, Il Natale di un'Idea," in *Amico Serafico,* XXXIII, 1 (1948), 1.

20. C. Lubich, "Questa è l'ora di S. Francesco, il Natale di un'Idea, " in *Amico Serafico,* XXXIII, 2 (1948), 12. Cf. in the same issue, C. Lubich, "Francescanesimo in atto," 5. "Only a solid and deep evangelical formation can keep alive an ideal society of fraternal love. There will certainly be this society among us, for as long as we are united Christ will be in our midst, and what he builds remains."

21. Cf. also LET March 30, 1948 ("Fratelli carissimi in Gesú . . ."); and LET May 11 1948 ("Carissimo Fratello in Gesú . . .").

22. LET February 27, 1948 ("Padre B . . .").

23. LET April 1, 1948 (Trent, Italy "Fratelli carissimi in Gesú . . ."). This letter, as in the one of March 30, 1948, contains the concept that Jesus in our midst consoles Jesus crucified and forsaken, "Because we are united, *we will have Him in our midst; Jesus who will be born through our unity will console our crucified Love!*"

24. LET April 29, 1948 ("Fratelli carissimi in Gesú . . .").

25. Igino Giordani, a writer and Italian congressman, had met Chiara at that time and remained in close ties with her. Cf. I. Giordani, *Diary of Fire,* (New York: New City Press, 1982), 38–42. Cf. also E. Robertson, *The Fire of Love, A Life of Igino Giordani 'Foco',* (London: New City, 1989), 157–177.

26. C. Lubich, "La Comunità Cristiana," in *Fides,* (October, 1948), 4. There is also a small pamphlet published at the end of 1949 with the *imprimatur* of Bishop Carlo de Ferrari, then bishop of Trent, Italy, entitled, *Un po' di storia del Movimento dell'unità* (hereafter *Un po' di storia*), that explains the history

of the newborn Movement. It reads: "Jesus was in the midst with his light and his love. We wanted him to be always present."

27. Cf. C. Lubich, *Jesus in the Midst*, (New York: New City Press, 1976), 15.

28. This fundamental document will be referred to as REC 1959 (Notes for Mariapolis talks).

29. C. Lubich, "Il nostro Ideale: Gesú in mezzo," in *Città Nuova*, III, 22 (1959), 2-3 (hereafter "Il nostro Ideale").

30. C. Lubich, *All One*, 79-91.

Chapter 1. What Is the Presence of Jesus in Our Midst and How Do We Partake in It

1. C. Lubich, "Il nostro Ideale," 2 and *All One*, 80. Already in a handwritten letter, "Lucerna del tuo corpo," published in *La Via* on November 12, 1949, Chiara states: "You cannot light up an environment—even if electric current is available—until two poles come into contact with one another. So too, is God's life in us, it must be shared so that it can radiate and bear witness to Christ."

2. See above in the Introduction, B.

3. This theme will be developed more extensively in Chapter 2.

4. WRIT 1949 (?) ("Come mai Gesú è in mezzo . . ."). The exact date of this writing is unknown, but it is presumed to be of the year 1949 or 1950. Cf. also REC November 18, 1961 (Grottaferrata, Italy), where she explains, "To have Jesus in our midst, it is not enough to love one another in the way you see it, because this love for one another must be understood in the way Jesus sees it; that is, being ready to give our lives."

5. C. Lubich, *Jesus in the Midst*, 37.

6. C. Lubich, *Jesus in the Midst*, 37–41. We will cite just a few lines to give an idea how Chiara makes use of these sources to confirm her own thought.

Basil: "Those who meet together in the name of someone else have to know well the will of the person who has gathered them together, and have to conform themselves to that will. . . ."

St. John Chrysostom: "In fact, Jesus is speaking of something more than simply meeting together . . . His words have this meaning: if anyone holds me as the principal motive of one's love for neighbor, then I will be with that person . . ."

Origen: "When Christ sees two or three gathered together in the faith of his name, he goes there, and remains in their midst, drawn by their faith and called forth by the unity of their minds."

Theodore the Studite: ". . . but to take care of your brothers so that you may also be loved by them, and that again you may love them in return, for in this way you will love and also be loved. In fact, where there is spiritual charity, there Christ is in the midst, as he promised."

7. WRIT 1950 (?) ("Non mirando . . ."), 10. This writing is in Chiara's own hand, and though uncompleted, it was circulated presumably in the years

1949–1950. This approximate date was deduced from the contents, ". . . for six years—since the Focolare began . . ." It has been published its entirety in English in the booklet, *A Little "Harmless" Manifesto* (New York: New City Press, 1973). The references cited in this study will come from the original stenciled text.

8. C. Lubich, *All One*, 49–50.

9. C. Lubich, *All One*, 79. In regards to the communion of goods, cf. C. Lubich, *When Our Love is Charity* (New York: New City Press, 1972), 34 (hereafter *Charity*), which reads: "Anyone who is not poor, at least spiritually, cannot hope to possess the kingdom of God, either in oneself or in communion with others." The following is included only in the Italian edition: "What was needed then was the kind of communion that generates, as we would say, the presence of Jesus in our midst."

10. WRIT December 2, 1946. And in LET November 6, 1947 Chiara also writes: "Be 'in him' [in your neighbor] in his sufferings, in his needs, in his fears, in his doubts, in his few moments of joy."

11. WRIT 1950 (?) ("Non Mirando . . ."), 11

12. Cf. C. Lubich, *Charity*, 23.

13. C. Lubich, *Meditations* (New York: New City Press, 1986), 81.

14. Cf. REC December 29, 1975 (Frascati, Italy).

15. Cf. REC April 13, 1955 (Milan), "Jesus in our midst mortifies your personal ideas, because you put them in common. More precisely, he shapes them rather than mortifies them, until they are no longer your ideas, nor your neighbor's, but the ideas of Jesus in your midst."

16. C. Lubich, "La legge di Loppiano" in *Città Nuova* XXIV, 14.

17. C. Lubich, *Charity*, 33.

18. WRIT May 16, 1950. And REC June 11, 1970 (Rocca di Papa, Italy), "To live Jesus in the focolare center, that is, to be always consumed in one, we must not only mortify ourselves, we must die to ourselves. Where God is found, human nature is not left alone; there is the 'new self', for the 'old self' has been crucified."

19. REC August 12, 1963 (Ala di Stura, Italy). And REC April 13, 1955 (Milan) "In putting Jesus in our midst, we have understood, that if we were truly thinking of our neighbor, we were, logically, poor of ourselves."

20. REC March 21, 1964 (Grottaferrata, Italy).

21. C. Lubich, *Colloqui Con I Gen* (Rome: Città Nuova, 1978), 184 (hereafter *Colloqui*).

22. C. Lubich, *All One*, 83. Elsewhere in REC February 26, 1964 (Grottaferrata, Italy), she said, "Consuming ourselves means that we truly give our soul, that our soul may emanate charity through living these negative virtues . . ."

23. C. Lubich, "Il nostro Ideale," 2.

24. C. Lubich, "Dialogo aperto. Perché Gesú sia sempre in mezzo a noi" in *Città Nuova*, XX, 3 (1976), 33 (hereafter Dialogo aperto), from the original talk: REC December 29, 1975 (Frascati, Italy, to the gen seminarians).

25. C. Lubich, *All One*, 82. Cf. also *id.*, "Dialogo aperto," 33.

26. C. Lubich, *All One*, 62.

27. WRIT December 12, 1963.

28. C. Lubich, "Dialogo aperto," 33. In the original talk, REC December 29, 1975 (Frascati, Italy, to the gen seminarians), Chiara gives concrete examples. Cf. also REC March 20, 1976 (Rocca di Papa, Italy).

29. C. Lubich, "Dialogo aperto," 33.

30. C. Lubich, "Dialogo aperto con i lettori" in *Città Nuova*, XX, 2 (1976), 33. Cf. REC December 30, 1975 (Rocca di Papa, Italy) and REC January 2, 1976 (Rocca di Papa, Italy, to the gen leaders).

31. C. Lubich, *Charity*, 55. Cf. REC December 30, 1975 (Rocca di Papa, Italy) and REC January 2, 1976 (Rocca di Papa, Italy, to the gen leaders), where she describes in familiar terms the particular method of the "moment of truth." Cf. also C. Lubich, "La legge di Loppiano," 27.

32. C. Lubich, "Chiara risponde ai gen" in *Gen*, X 2/3, p. 1, from the original talk: REC January 2, 1976 (Rocca di Papa, Italy, to the gen leaders).

33. C. Lubich, *A Call to Love—Spiritual Writings, Volume 1* (New York: New City Press, 1989), 105 (hereafter *A Call to Love*).

34. WRIT November 4, 1962. For the relationship of Jesus in our midst with the eucharist, see ahead in Chapter 3, B, "Jesus in our midst and the eucharist."

35. C. Lubich, *All One*, 83–84. And REC February 26, 1964 (Grottaferrata, Italy), "At times, when reading the gospel, we ought to take note of what Jesus did *not* say (as in this case) . . . because he did not specify who, so the 'two or three' can be anyone."

36. LET 1957 (?).

37. REC March 21, 1964 (Grottaferrata, Italy).

38. C. Lubich, *Jesus in the Midst*, 39. In reading this passage, REC November 27, 1975 (Loppiano, to the citizens of the Permanent Mariapolis), Chiara adds: "He is present even when we are distant from one another, if, however, we were first in agreement . . . and if we had also established a way of life similar to that of a focolarino." Cf. also REC December 29, 1975 (Frascati, Italy).

39. See ahead, Chapter 3.

40. C. Lubich, *All One*, 81. Cf. also REC February 26, 1964 (Grottaferrata, Italy) and REC December 7, 1964 (Nuremberg, to a group of Evangelical pastors).

41. C. Lubich, *Yes, Yes, No, No* (London: New City, 1977), 87.

42. C. Lubich, "Dialogo aperto. La presenza di Gesú fra noi," in *Città Nuova*, XXII, 1 (1978), 41 from REC November 27, 1975 (Loppiano, to the citizens of the Permanent Mariapolis).

43. REC 1959 (Notes for Mariapolis talks). These effects are also connected with the fruits of the spirit which St. Paul speaks about, from the same recording, "We had recognized that in our life of communion, in that little community of ours which shared this ideal, and also in our own selves, when there was charity, there were also present all the consequential effects which

St. Paul speaks of: light, joy, peace, serenity. When charity was missing, everything lost its meaning."

44. C. Lubich, *All One*, 80. Cf. also REC February 26, 1964 (Grottaferrata, Italy).

45. C. Lubich, *All One*, 85.

46. REC February 26, 1964 (Grottaferrata, Italy).

47. C. Lubich, *All One*, 81–82. And REC June 12, 1960 (Grottaferrata, Italy), "Our mere human senses or our physical senses do not detect God's presence among us, but as certain mystics say, it can be felt by the senses of the soul . . ."

48. C. Lubich, *All One*, 82.

49. WRIT 1950 (?) ("Non mirando . . ."), 9. And C. Lubich, "Gli Albori" in the supplement to *Città Nuova*, III, 22 (1959), 2 (hereafter "Gli Albori"), "Through his grace, the sacred scriptures, especially the gospel, acquired a new flavor"; REC December 7, 1964 (Nuremberg, to a group of Evangelical pastors), "We understood the gospel in a new way, as words of life, words meant for everyone."

50. C. Lubich, *All One*, 88.

51. C. Lubich, *Jesus in the Midst*, 44.

52. C. Lubich, *A Call to Love*, 107.

53. LET March 4, 1950 (Trent, Italy, "Signor P . . .").

54. DIAR August 15, 1970.

55. C. Lubich, *Colloqui*, 87.

56. C. Lubich, *All One*, 90.

57. C. Lubich, *Diary 1964/65*, (New York: New City Press, 1987), 6. Cf. REC December 16, 1965 (Rocca di Papa, Italy).

58. C. Lubich, *Jesus in the Midst*, 45. In describing the Focolare's beginnings, REC May 24, 1971 (Loppiano), Chiara says: "The only light I had to go ahead on was present when we lit this lantern of Jesus in our midst. In other words, imagine if all the lights were out, and there was only one little candle in the world. This little candle was my light; it was Jesus in our midst, who enabled us to understand how God wanted us to go ahead."

59. C. Lubich, *Meditations*, 123.

60. C. Lubich, *Colloqui*, 13 and cf. also *Detti Gen*, 34.

61. WRIT 1963 (?) ("Figliola, che cosa desideri?"), found also in *All One*, 33.

62. See above in this same Chapter and section.

63. C. Lubich, *Jesus in the Midst*, 45–46.

64. See above in this same Chapter and section.

65. WRIT 1959 (?) ("Non mirando . . ."), 13. And REC February 26, 1964 (Grottaferrata, Italy), "This is why we had the strength to stay with it and not go back home, because we had a Brother among us, a divine Brother, more brother to us than we were to ourselves."

66. REC June 17, 1969 (Rocca di Papa, Italy, to a group of Orthodox).

67. C. Lubich, "Il nostro Ideale," 2.

68. LET February 14, 1952 (Vigo di fasso, Italy, "Carissimi Focolarini e Focolarine . . .").

69. See above, Introduction, B.

70. See above in this same Chapter and section.

71. C. Lubich, "Dialogo aperto. Perché Lui sia fra noi parlare o amare?" in *Città Nuova*, XX, 6 (1976), 37. And REC March 21, 1964 (Grottaferrata, Italy), "Jesus in our midst, in the Mystical Body, in my opinion, is to a cell of the Mystical Body what health is to the human body. Before we met this Ideal, life was so dull and boring, so tasteless, that we were never satisfied with anything. With this Ideal, however, at a given point we experienced a certain fullness. The truth is before we were ill, and now we have regained our health."

72. REC March 21, 1964 (Grottaferrata, Italy).

73. C. Lubich, *All One*, 86. Cf. also REC July 25, 1960 (Grottaferrata, Italy) and REC February 26, 1964 (Grottaferrata, Italy).

74. WRIT 1949 ("San Giovanni della Croce . . .").

75. REC September 17, 1961 (Grottaferrata, Italy).

76. C. Lubich, *Detti Gen*, 27 and cf. *Colloqui*, 80. Elsewhere, in REC April 2, 1961, she had explained, "being in our midst—'show me your friends and I will tell you who you are'—Jesus infects us, he makes us live as other Christs." And in REC July 25, 1960, "They will sense that sanctity is God himself, that it is Jesus; he is the Saint, and having found him again in their midst, they will discover the most direct way to sanctity."

77. C. Lubich, "Dialogo aperto. Il mordente dei primi cristiani" in *Città Nuova*, XX, 15/16 (1976), 33.

78. *Scr. Sp./1*, 284.

79. C. Lubich, *All One*, 79–80. And WRIT 1949 (?) ("San Giovanni della Croce . . ."). Individual sanctity is not enough for us, we want the sanctification of Jesus among us, of Jesus-us." On this theme, see ahead to Chapter 2, A.

80. C. Lubich, "La legge di Loppiano" 27.

81. LET February 27, 1948 ("Padre B. . . .").

82. LET June 1949 (Rome, "Carissimi Fratelli e Sorelle nell'Unità . . ."). Cf. Jn 14:2.

83. C. Lubich, "La comunità cristiana" 4.

84. C. Lubich, "La comunità cristiana" 4. And REC September 1969 (Rocca di Papa, Italy), "In the early days we had abolished the term apostolate because we would say that we had to love God and keep Jesus in our midst; the one who truly lived the apostolate was Jesus in our midst, because only God can bring others to conversion."

85. WRIT 1950 (?) ("Non mirando . . ."). And LET January 7, 1971 (Rocca di Papa, Italy, "Carissimi focolarini sposati . . ."), "Jesus in our midst was at work and not rarely did the light strike and blind souls as if on a new way to Damascus."

86. C. Lubich, *All One*, 86–87. In addressing a community who lives with "Jesus in its midst" Chiara repeats in WRIT-REC March 28, 1972 (Loppiano, Italy) this powerful conviction: "Because Christ is present, whoever comes with a sincere heart, and is searching, *finds* Christ, because . . . *he is there*."

87. C. Lubich, "Dialogo aperto. Affinché il mondo creda" in *Città Nuova*, XX, 8 (1976), 35.

88. REC September 17, 1961 (Grottaferrata, Italy).

89. C. Lubich, "Dialogo aperto. Tutto è nato da due scelte di fondo" in *Città Nuova*, XXI, 13 (1977), 41.

90. *Opera di Maria. Statuti (Statutes of the Work of Mary)*, (Rome, 1962) n. 91, 43. The official statutes of the Work of Mary have since been revised and updated by Chiara, and reapproved by the Church on June 29, 1990. Being that this book was written prior to this, references throughout it in regards to the statutes will be to those noted above.

91. WRIT September 11, 1950. And REC February 26, 1964, "Before, I wasn't so aware that people could convert so quickly. We were individuals, perhaps even good ones, but we were not united in a way that Jesus could live among us. How could we have converted others in such a way?"

92. LET July 20, 1976 (Sierre, Switzerland, "Carissimi Gen . . .").

93. C. Lubich, *All One*, 18; cf. also, 87.

94. Cf. C. Lubich, "Gli Albori," 2 and REC July 17, 1960 (Grottaferrata, Italy).

95. C. Lubich, *Jesus in the Midst*, 58. The term *consenserint* is the Latin for "who are in agreement" from Mt 18:19. Cf. also *All One*, 87.

96. C. Lubich, *Jesus in the Midst*, 58. And REC 1959 (Notes for Mariapolis talks), "It was logical, since we were united in his name, the presence of Jesus was established among us; thus, it is Jesus who asks the Father, and who obtains from the Father."

97. C. Lubich, *Jesus in the Midst*, 58–59.

98. C. Lubich, *Jesus in the Midst*, 59. And LET July 20, 1976 (Sierre, Switzerland, "Carissimi Gen . . ."), "United in the name of Jesus you will ask both the possible and the impossible, and you will see them happen as though they were the most normal realities."

99. C. Lubich, *Jesus in the Midst*, 60.

100. REC December 30, 1975 (Rocca di Papa, Italy).

101. REC April 12, 1966 (Rocca di Papa, Italy, to a group of Anglicans). And REC February 26, 1964 (Grottaferrata, Italy), "Unity is a consequence of the presence of Jesus in our midst; Jesus in our midst is a consequence of mutual charity and mutual charity is a consequence of charity."

102. C. Lubich, *All One*, 81.

103. REC 1959 (Notes for Mariapolis talks).

104. C. Lubich, *All One*, 81. And REC July 25, 1960, "There is no one who can accomplish his testament for the world, no disciple has that capability, nor will any saint ever have it; only he himself, he living in our midst will be the one to fulfill his testament, only he will make all people one."

105. REC December 7, 1964 (Nuremberg, Germany, to a group of Evangelical pastors).

106. C. Lubich, *Jesus in the Midst*, 15; cf. also "Dialogo aperto. La presenza di Gesú fra noi," mentioned in section B of this Chapter. The original talk,

REC November 27, 1975 (Loppiano, Italy, to the citizens of the Permanent Mariapolis), continues, "It is he, in person! He is present. For example, there must be, I don't know, 700 of us here. But we are not 700 at all, we are 701. Because he is present. This presence of his I would say almost scares me; I am afraid to speak knowing that he is listening. But since this is also his will for me, I think that he is pleased for the little I do for him . . . He has been to this earth, and has seen our limitations. He knows how little we are, and how narrow are our thoughts. He knows us, therefore. He is not only God, for thus he would be unreachable. He is human. He is in the midst of us as Jesus."

107. WRIT Christmas 1974.

108. WRIT September 20, 1961. And REC June 8, 1965 (Rocca di Papa, Italy, ecumenical meeting: "Spiritualità del Movimento dei Focolari"), "He knew that if they loved one another as he had loved them, he would remain in their midst; thus, the nostalgia that had already taken hold of them, causing their sadness at his departure, would have been at least alleviated to some degree. So at the end he gave them this commandment that sums up all the others, that he might be able to remain spiritually present in their midst."

109. WRIT 1949 ("Lucerna del tuo corpo . . ."). Cf. C. Lubich, *Meditations*, 36, and *Jesus in the Midst*, 41–43, which describes the historical context out of which these concepts emerged ("in a warm, filial talk that I had with the then Monsignor Montini . . ."). For the value given to Jesus in our midst see also above, Introduction, B.

110. C. Lubich, *Colloqui*, 184.

111. C. Lubich, *Diary 1964/65*, 164.

112. C. Lubich, *Jesus in the Midst*, 20.

113. REC May 24 1971 (Loppiano, Italy to the focolarini).

114. REC October 21, 1975 (Rocca di Papa, Italy). Cf. also REC March 17, 1975 (Frascati, Italy, to the Priest's School).

115. See above in A, "How to reestablish Jesus in our midst."

116. C. Lubich, *Meditations*, 104.

117. REC November 18, 1961 (Grottaferrata, Italy). And REC December 16, 1965 (Rocca di Papa, Italy, to a gathering of priests), "Jesus in our midst is by all means an added grace, and obviously, a new presence of Jesus."

118. C. Lubich, *Jesus in the Midst*, 70–71.

119. LET May 11, 1948 ("Carissimo Fratello in Gesú . . .").

120. LET February 17, 1949 ("Fratelli nostri nell'Unità . . .").

121. WRIT 1950 (?) ("Non mirando . . ."), 9–10. And REC February 26, 1964 (Grottaferrata, Italy), "The expression 'in our midst' intends to mean that he is in us, that he makes us one."

122. REC April 13, 1955 (Milan). And REC December 20, 1966 (Rocca di Papa, Italy), "He takes us into himself, we are in him in our midst."

123. REC November 18, 1961 (Grottaferrata, Italy). And REC Summer 1955 (Vigo di Fassa, Italy), "He is in us and he possesses us"; REC June 8, 1965 (Rocca di Papa, Italy, ecumenical meeting), "It is our wish for all of Christianity: that he be present, that he take us into himself, that we be an expression of him alone."

124. REC March 21, 1964 (Grottaferrata, Italy).

125. C. Lubich, *Yes, Yes, No, No*, 71.

126. REC November 18, 1961 (Grottaferrata, Italy).

127. C. Lubich, *Meditations*, 34.

128. *Opera di Maria, Statuti* (Rome, 1962), 7–8.

129. REC July 7, 1962. (Grottaferrata, Italy).

130. See above, note 72.

131. LET February 21, 1964 (Rome, "Carissima Madre M.T. . . .").

132. LET November 6, 1947 ("Carissime sorelline . . .").

133. C. Lubich, "Un po' di storia," 7.

134. WRIT 1950 (?) ("Non mirando . . ."), 10. And REC April 2, 1961, ". . . where Jesus in our midst might be triumphant, and where our ego, of whatever kind, might be purified by this fire and might also share in this fire."

135. See above in A of this same Chapter, "How to reestablish the presence of Jesus in our midst when it is lacking."

136. WRIT 1963 (?) ("Figliola, che cosa desideri?") found also in *All One*, 34. In the original, instead of "we have the fire itself," it reads, "we draw from the fire directly."

137. See above in B of this same Chapter, "Jesus in our midst brings about conversions."

138. C. Lubich, *Diary 1964/65*, 145.

139. LET February 17, 1949 ("Fratelli nostri nell'Unità . . .").

140. REC July 25, 1960 (Grottaferrata, Italy).

141. WRIT 1963 (?) ("Figliola, che cosa desideri?") found also in *All One*, 34. The original shows some variations.

142. C. Lubich, *Yes, Yes, No, No*, 65. Also in the following phrase in DIAR November 7, 1968, ". . . while we moved into the incorruptible and eternal house; *Jesus in the eucharist,* in whom we enter each morning, *Jesus in our midst,* who envelopes us in everywhere on earth."

143. C. Lubich, *Diary 1964/65*, 47.

144. WRIT 1949 (?) ("San Giovanni della Croce . . ."). And REC July 29, 1960 (Grottaferrata, Italy), " 'Where there is charity and love, there is God.' God will be in our midst and will accomplish his will, his kingdom will come, and will be perfect, as perfect as humanly possible, but it will be the kingdom of God."

145. WRIT 1962 (?) ("E nacque il Focolare . . .").

146. C. Lubich, "Il nostro ideale," 2–3, also in *All One*, 84, with a slight variation.

147. Cf. REC July 29, 1960 (Grottaferrata, Italy) and REC April 13, 1955 (Milan), "I renounce everything so that Christ may triumph in our midst, that the kingdom of God may be present, where he reigns over all our powers, from our intelligence, to our heart, our will, and our strength . . . and our entire physical selves."

148. *Scr. Sp./1*, 284.

149. WRIT 1963 (?) ("Figliola, che cosa desideri?"). In modified form in *All One*, 33.

150. DIAR May 11, 1971

151. WRIT 1951 ("L'Ordine di Maria e il suo Ideale").

Chapter 2. The Profound Reality of Jesus in Our Midst

1. REC April 13, 1955 (Milan).

2. REC August 20, 1965 (Ala di Stura, Italy [?]).

3. REC January 1, 1969 (Rocca di Papa, Italy). Elsewhere, in REC March 15, 1975 (Rocca di Papa, Italy), Chiara describes this experience of the "Soul" as the fulfillment of Jesus' words, "That they may be one as you and I are one," through the one Christ who lives on the nothingness of two or more persons. "Our nothingness and Christ in us."

4. C. Lubich, *All One*, 4. And REC July 4, 1974 (Rocca di Papa, Italy), "If the kingdom of God is here among us because we are united in his name, is it more of a miracle to see him or not to see him? For me it is more of a miracle not to see him. So, what did I see in 1949? I saw the reality that was present there . . . Jesus in our midst was opened to us and I saw where we were. Jesus in our midst embraced us, God embraced us . . . but simply, I just saw the reality that was there."

5. Transcription of a conversation of October 2, 1955, where it is also stated: "When we are consumed in one through Jesus in our midst, we are a single entity, and this entity is united to Christ the head, and to Mary, and with the communion of saints, because the primary truth is unity."

6. See above, Introduction, B and Chapter 1, A, "The conditions."

7. WRIT December 2, 1946. ("L'Unità").

8. WRIT December 12, 1946 ("L'Unità").

9. WRIT December 12, 1946 ("L'Unità").

10. WRIT 1949 (?) ("Come mai Gesú è in mezzo a noi . . ."). And C. Lubich, "Dialogo aperto. Solitudine e unità" in *Città Nuova*, XIX, 11 (1975), 33, "On the other hand, the life of unity among Christians is not true if it is not composed of many Christs, of many persons who are no longer themselves, but Christ in them. God in them. Unity does not exist in any other way. Unity exists only between God and God."

11. LET May 11, 1948 ("Carissimo Fratello in Gesú . . .").

12. WRIT 1958 ("Appunti di Regola").

13. See above in Chapter 1, B, "Jesus in our midst brings about conversions," and C. Lubich, "La Rivoluzione Cristiana" in *Gen's*, I, 5 (1971), 1, "He didn't look toward the people of this world, perhaps they would not have understood him. He looked toward the Father, because the bond of this unity is God, who gives us the grace for us to be one."

14. See above in this same Chapter.

15. WRIT 1949. And REC December 29, 1975 (Frascati, Italy), "When he is in our midst, we are one single Jesus, but at the same time we are also three Jesus' "

16. WRIT March 27, 1950 (Lido di Ostia, Italy). And REC June 29, 1968 (Rocca di Papa, Italy), "Therefore the human personality is not only emptied

out by the divine, it is also empowered in a supernatural way, in a divine way. . . . You will become so different from one another while at the same time identical, because you will be Jesus, somewhat a copy of who he is in the Holy Trinity. God is Father, God is Son, God is Holy Spirit. One God, yet three distinct persons. This is how we will be: many distinct personalities, as the saints are, yet all one, because Christ will live in all."

17. C. Lubich, *Charity*, 21.

18. WRIT November 6, 1949. And WRIT 1950 ("Ho osservato . . ."), "I saw that every two souls establish a trinity. . . . And that every trinity composed is different from the other, from every other—a heaven of its own. How many heavens, therefore, are there in unity, how many beautiful aspects of Jesus."

19. C. Lubich, "Sintesi della spiritualità" in *Mariapoli '68* (Rome, 1968), 76. The original recording is REC June 8, 1965 (Rocca di Papa, Italy, ecumenical meeting).

20. WRIT September 29, 1950. To be noted here is the strong ecclesiastical accent. This trinitarian life which is the fulfillment of Jesus' new commandment, is no other than "the mystical life of the Church," the Mystical Body of Christ. We will cover this aspect more fully further ahead.

21. WRIT July 25, 1949. And REC May 13, 1970 (Loppiano, Italy), "Because love is something that consumes itself like a candle, and therefore, *is not*; however, in the very moment it *is not*, it *is love*."

22. REC May 13, 1970 (Loppiano, Italy).

23. REC May 13, 1970 (Loppiano, Italy).

24. WRIT September 2, 1949. Cf. *Scr. Sp./1*, 140.

25. REC Summer 1955 (Vigo di Fassa, Italy).

26. Cf. her reference to *Divinum illud*, ahead in this same Chapter, C and DIAR February 8, 1981, "It is he, in fact, who binds in unity the members of the Mystical Body." She also said in REC November 25, 1961: "Now, the unity of which we speak, which is the unity of the Mystical Body, but also explicit and sometimes seen and felt in its effects, is the work of the Holy Spirit."

27. See above, in this same Chapter, A.

28. WRIT September 29, 1950. "Having been made God" in the sense of the process of individual and collective "divinization" by work of the Holy Spirit. "Divinization" as said above, is more specifically "Christification."

29. WRIT 1950 (?) ("San Giovanni della Croce . . .").

30. WRIT 1950 (?) ("San Giovanni della Croce . . .").

31. REC June 23, 1974 (Rocca di Papa, Italy), "It is he who makes us other Jesus', he who makes of us a collective Jesus, a mystical Jesus"; REC February 9, 1979 (Albano, Italy), "Through this charism we establish the presence of Jesus in us and the presence of Jesus in our midst; this is one of the works of the Holy Spirit."

32. REC March 14, 1975 (Rocca di Papa, Italy).

33. See ahead in Chapter 3, A, "The importance of being engrafted into the hierarchical Church."

34. REC September 7, 1961.

35. REC April 2, 1961.

36. Cf. REC June 10, 1973 (Rocca di Papa, Italy), where she compares Pentecost—when the group of disciples "became Church, when they became a family, [because] the Holy Spirit bound them and they became something new: full of strength, full of power, full of God's Word"—to the experience of the Focolare with Jesus in our midst.

37. REC June 12, 1960, "This presence of God that existed in the first Christian communities, the reason for which it was said that the breath of the Holy Spirit was moving there, should also exist in a certain way in the focolare center. Jesus must be present in our midst"

38. REC November 11, 1966 (Rocca di Papa, Italy). Fr. Leone Veuthey, O.F.M. met Chiara at the end of 1946. Chiara underlines the christological aspect of our "divinization," as she also does in the following text which is a transcription of a recording of October 2, 1955: "Today I said that I and another person form a particular Christ, and also distinctly we form a Christ; precisely Christ, not his Spirit, because there also involves the faculty of reason, etc."

39. REC December 8, 1975 (Rocca di Papa, Italy). And in the same talk Chiara concludes: "But Jesus is present. The important thing is that Jesus is present; whether dressed in pontifical attire, or as a king, or a little boy, he is still Jesus."

40. WRIT March 27, 1950 (Lido di Ostia, Italy).

41. REC December 29, 1975 (Frascati, Italy). And REC November 27, 1975 (Loppiano, Italy, to the citizens of the Permanent Mariapolis), "Therefore, when we have Jesus in our midst, we have the Holy Spirit in our midst. This is why our lives are enlightened on the steps to take to go ahead."

42. Cf. C. Lubich, *All One*, 57–68 and *Meditations*, 24–29.

43. C. Lubich, "Cristo nella comunità" 40–41 and WRIT-REC March 29, 1978 (Rocca di Papa, Italy, ecumenical meeting).

44. LET January 2, 1945 (?) ("Carissime sorelline . . .").

45. LET August 14, 1948 (Trent, Italy "Rev. Padre . . ."). And LET February 17, 1949 ("Fratelli nostri nell'Unità . . ."), "Unity becomes a vague dream or a wild fancy if the person who seeks it does not hold as one's everything: *Jesus, forsaken by all, even by his Father.*"

46. WRIT August 28, 1949.

47. WRIT-REC December 8, 1971 (Rocca di Papa, Italy).

48. *Opera di Maria, Statuti* (Rome, 1962), 9. In commenting on this rule, REC December 5, 1966 (Rocca di Papa, Italy), Chiara underlines that the Church, by approving it, has confirmed this relationship. "It gives us the key, it tells us what to do, it gives us support, it gives us a means by which, if we follow it, we can always have Jesus in our midst . . . It tells us, 'you will always have Jesus in your midst if you will always have love for the Cross, for Jesus crucified and forsaken' ." The relationship between Jesus Forsaken and unity is already very clear in all of the preceding attempts of formulating the rule. Cf. for example "Appunti di Regola," 1958: ". . . to live this divine engrafting into Christ, and through him into our brothers and sisters, the soul of the

focolarini must always be cut at a living portion, at its portion that is most alive. They must know how to place unity first. The focolarini succeed in this purpose inasmuch as they always have as their model the one they have chosen, and to whom they have consecrated themselves—Jesus Crucified and Forsaken." Cf. also "Compendio di Alcune Norme Fondamentali da servire per le constituzioni dell'istituto secolare 'Cuore Immacolato di Maria' " (Compendium of some basic norms to follow for the constitutions of the secular institute "The Immaculate Heart of Mary") (1959), notes 37–38.

49. WRIT 1962 (?) ("E nacque il Focolare . . .").

50. REC November 27, 1975 (Loppiano, Italy, to the citizens of the permanent Mariapolis). And REC December 30, 1975 (Rocca di Papa, Italy), "To have Jesus in our midst, it is necessary to live Jesus forsaken, meaning to be nothing, to be love. Therefore, Jesus forsaken, even if lived in terms of oneself . . . afterward becomes the means for having Jesus in our midst."

51. WRIT-REC December 8, 1971 (Rocca di Papa, Italy). This passage was taken, with some alteration, from a preceding text, LET October 1, 1958.

52. C. Lubich, *All One*, 71.

53. WRIT-REC December 8, 1971 (Rocca di Papa, Italy) and WRIT 1950 (?) ("Non mirando . . .").

54. LET February 4, 1962 (Rome, "Carissimo C. . . .").

55. See above Chapter 1, A, "How to reestablish the presence of Jesus in our midst when it is lacking."

56. LET February 4, 1962 (Rome, "Carissimo C. . . .").

57. DIAR March 11, 1970.

58. WRIT 1951 ("L'Ordine di Maria e il suo Ideale"), where the following is cited: (a) "He . . . [is] personally present in all the mystical members, and acts in them in a divine way" (Pius XII, *Mystici Corporis* AAS, XXXV, 219); (b) "Even more, we will always be more united with God and with Christ in the measure that we will be members one of the other and mindful of one another, as on the other hand, the closer we are to God and to our divine head in ardent love, the greater we will be united and fused by way of charity" (Pius XII, *Mystici Corporis* AAS, XXV, 229).

Chapter 3. Ecclesiological and Sociological Aspects of Jesus in Our Midst

1. Cf. C. Lubich, "Un po' di storia"; *All One*, 41 and *Servants of All* (New York: New City Press, 1978), 79–85. Also the following phrase in LET February 14, 1952, " 'Oh, my little children, love one another *as* I have loved you' and remain obedient to the Church to the point of death, death on the cross. Only in this way, in the unity among yourselves and with the Church, will this Ideal invade the world."

2. WRIT 1950 (?) ("Non mirando . . ."), 18, although here shown in a form included in a prepared talk, WRIT-REC December 8, 1971 (Rocca di Papa, Italy). And C. Lubich, *Jesus in the Midst*, 27–28, "What was it that gave such

importance to Jesus in our midst, whom we tried to have present in all our gatherings, if not the faith and the conviction that he was there in our midst because our little group was united to the great Church and to its shepherds?"

3. Cf. REC September 7, 1961 (Grottaferrata, Italy) where Chiara recounts this episode. In the same talk she says, "If our Movement is united to the Church, as it wants to be . . . to the point of losing its own spirituality should the Church see it as not appropriate . . . we can have hope that the members at the Center of the Focolare will be vivified . . . by the presence of Jesus, the invisible head of the Church."

4. See above in Chapter 1, B, "Jesus in our midst enlightens."

5. C. Lubich, *All One*, 88. REC 1959 (notes for Mariapolis talks), "This is so because Jesus who lives in our midst is no other than Jesus of the Church, Jesus who lives in the Holy Father and in the bishops." And C. Lubich, *Servants of All*, 82. "The more we have Jesus present in our midst, through this Ideal we live, the more we understand the beauty of what the Church hierarchy tells us."

6. C. Lubich, *All One*, 88.

7. C. Lubich, *All One*, 88.

8. C. Lubich, *Servants of All*, 83.

9. REC June 28, 1969 (Rocca di Papa, Italy).

10. WRIT-REC December 8, 1971 (Rocca di Papa, Italy).

11. See above in Chapter 1, C, "A presence that presupposes the collectivity."

12. REC July 7, 1962 (Grottaferrata, Italy).

13. WRIT October 3, 1950 (Rome). And WRIT 1950 (?) ("Non mirando . . ."), "Reciprocal love, therefore, had bound in unity the members of the Mystical Body, who (already united by grace), in the perfect supernatural life caused by the perfect correspondence to grace, felt this life circulate within themselves; they felt filled by the one spirit." By "perfect" Chiara here intends the meaning found in 1 Jn 4:12–13, which she cites immediately afterward.

14. WRIT October 3, 1950 (Rome).

15. REC January 31, 1969 (Rocca di Papa, Italy, to a gathering of priests).

16. REC October 20, 1975 (Rocca di Papa, Italy). The words of the Pope Paul VI cited by C. Lubich, in *Jesus in the Midst*, 79–80, are: "Are the faithful united in love, in the charity of Christ? Then certainly this is a living parish, here is the true Church, since then there is a flourishing of that divine and human phenomenon which perpetuates the presence of Christ among us. Or do the faithful gather only because they are listed in the parish register or recorded in the baptismal files? Do they gather only to hear Sunday mass, without getting to know one another, maybe even elbowing one another out of the way? If so, the Church in this case does not appear bound together; the cement, which must bind all members into a real, organic unity, is not yet at work . . .

"Remember the solemn words of Christ. They will truly recognize you as my disciples, as authentic faithful and followers, if you love one another, if there is this warmth of affection and sentiment; if there is a vibrant sympathy for the others. A sympathy not merely passively experienced but deliberately willed, not merely spontaneously arising but purposely achieved, with that breadth of heart and power of begetting Jesus in our midst which spring from an awareness of our unity in him and through him."

17. REC July 7, 1962 (Grottaferrata, Italy).

18. REC June 17, 1971 (Rocca di Papa, Italy). Here is an explanation, from REC June 3, 1972 (Rocca di Papa, Italy), "We understood that we were Church, 'Church-material', and we could even say 'the Church' because realities in God are entirely different from human realities . . . I can explain it in this way: on earth there are the dimensions of space and time, while in the beyond there is no space or time. In the midst of that group of souls that we were, we supposed there to be also the presence of the Holy Father, the presence of the bishops, of all Catholics, of all baptized Christians, of all whom God sees as the Church in the past . . . all the way to the end of the world. For the reason that we supposed this fact, we were Church; but in heaven, what is supposed is already present."

19. C. Lubich, *Yes, Yes, No, No*, 88. Chiara expesses the same, in REC June 27, 1967 (Rocca di Papa, Italy), in these terms, "Wherever we are spread about in the world or whoever we are . . . if we have Christ in our midst, there we have the Church! But take note: it is not just a part of the Church. No. It is the Church! Just as it is for a particle of the sacred host." Cf. also REC December 29, 1975 (Frascati, Italy).

20. *Scr. Sp/2*, 144.

21. C. Lubich, *Jesus in the Midst*, 22.

22. C. Lubich, *Jesus in the Midst*, 23. Chiara explains elsewhere, in REC January 31, 1969 (Rocca di Papa, Italy, to a gathering of priests), "In Africa, for example, there are lay people alone, who, through their testimony, have brought Christ to others. Afterward, a priest is needed to reap what has been sown, but the point is that Jesus in our midst, spiritually present, bears witness to himself. . . . That pagan people believed and asked to be baptized for they had seen the unity lived in this group of laypersons."

23. REC October 20, 1975 (Rocca di Papa, Italy).

24. REC March 17, 1975 (Frascati, Italy, to the school for priests).

25. WRIT 1950 (?) ("Non mirando . . ."), 19.

26. C. Lubich, *L'Eucaristia* (Rome: Città Nuova, 1977), 110.

27. C. Lubich, *L'Eucaristia*, 83–89.

28. C. Lubich, *Diary 1964/65*, 116.

29. *Scr. Sp./1*, 141.

30. REC January 31, 1969 (Rocca di Papa, Italy). And REC July 25, 1960 (Grottaferrata, Italy), "And if the sacraments were abolished, how could we not drink from the fountain of living water which is the living charity among us, Christ in our midst?"

31. See "Ecumenism, the eucharist, and Jesus in our midst."

32. WRIT 1958 ("Appunti di Regola, Opera di Maria"), 46.

33. C. Lubich, *All One*, 77. And REC November 29, 1974 (Rocca di Papa, Italy, at a gathering of men from various religious orders), "Since charity is

143

always enlightening, each person becomes enlightened about one's own vocation . . . and thus becomes always more Benedictine, or Franciscan, or always more Dominican."

34. REC June 8, 1965 (Rocca di Papa, Italy, ecumenical meeting).

35. LET April 15, 1971 (Rocca di Papa, Italy, "Carissime Suore . . .").

36. C. Lubich, *Jesus in the Midst*, 76.

37. REC May 15, 1965 (Loppiano, Italy).

38. REC March 31, 1979 (Frascati, Italy).

39. C. Lubich, *Jesus in the Midst*, 71. Here Chiara also cites Cyril of Alexandria, who in speaking of the Council of Nicea states, "Certainly together with them sat Christ himself, Christ who said: 'Where two or three are gathered together in my name, there am I in the midst of them.' " Also on the same page she cites John Chrysostom, Leontius, and John Damascene.

40. C. Lubich, *Jesus in the Midst*, 71.

41. Cf. C. Lubich, *Jesus in the Midst*, 74–79.

42. C. Lubich, *Jesus in the Midst*, 74.

43. C. Lubich, *Jesus in the Midst*, 78.

44. DIAR June 3, 1967.

45. REC December 8, 1975 (Rocca di Papa, Italy).

46. REC December 8, 1975 (Rocca di Papa, Italy).

47. Cf. C. Lubich, *All One*, 19–25.

48. LET April 29, 1948 ("Fratelli carissimi in Gesú . . .").

49. WRIT Pentecost 1965 (Introduction to the ecumenical meeting).

50. The narration of this episode is taken from REC March 21, 1964 (Grottaferrata, Italy). It is important to remember that in the time this occurred (1960), the ecumenical question was not widely felt in Italy.

51. REC January 31, 1969 (Rocca di Papa, Italy, at a gathering of priests).

52. REC November 17, 1965 (Liverpool, to a group of Anglicans).

53. REC November 17, 1965 (Liverpool, to a group of Anglicans).

54. REC May 8, 1970 (Rocca di Papa, Italy, to a gathering of the Reformed Church).

55. C. Lubich, "Cristo nella comunità" and REC March 29, 1978 (Rocca di Papa, Italy, to a group of Anglicans). Cf. also C. Lubich, *Jesus in the Midst*, 78.

56. REC May 8, 1970 (Rocca di Papa, Italy, to a group of the Reformed Church).

57. REC May 3, 1969 (Loppiano, Italy). Speaking to a group of Orthodox Catholics on Jesus in our midst, REC February 15, 1968 (Istanbul, Turkey), Chiara says, "As we are not able to share the eucharistic communion together, let's in the meantime share a spiritual communion. The day will come when we will share the eucharistic one."

58. REC December 7, 1964 (Nuremberg, Germany, to a group of Evangelical pastors).

59. C. Lubich, *All One*, 21. Cf. also C. Lubich, "Che tutti siano uno," in *Città Nuova*, XI, 18 (1967), 16 and REC November 17, 1965 (Liverpool, to a group of Anglicans).

60. REC May 8, 1970 (Rocca di Papa, Italy, to a group of the Reformed Church).

61. C. Lubich, "Cristo nella comunità," 40. And *Mariapoli '68,* 80, that summarizes the concepts in REC February 15, 1969 (Istanbul, Turkey, to a group of Orthodox), "After living for a long while the practice of mutual love, it became logical to begin to speak also about theological matters. By that time we were speaking as brothers and sisters, because our love had been proven through our life together. Jesus in our midst, to whom all entrusted themselves, because he is the truth, helped to resolve little by little many issues."

62. REC June 16, 1967 (Rocca di Papa, Italy).

63. REC May 23, 1976 (Rocca di Papa, Italy, to a group of the Reformed Church). For an example of a dialogue of this kind cf. REC May 8, 1970 (Rocca di Papa, Italy, to a group of the reformed Church) and REC May 21, 1970 (Rocca di Papa, Italy, to a group of Evangelicals).

64. C. Lubich, *All One,* 25. Cf. also REC January 21, 1967 (Canterbury, to a group of various Anglican denominations) and REC June 1967 (Istanbul, Turkey, to a group of Orthodox).

65. REC May 8, 1971 (London, to a group of Anglicans).

66. C. Lubich, "Dialogo aperto. Unità delle Chiese," in *Città Nuova,* XIX, 12 (1975), 33 and WRIT-REC March 27, 1974 (Rocca di Papa, Italy, to the citizens of Loppiano, Italy).

67. C. Lubich, "Questa è l'ora di S. Francesco, il Natale di un'Idea," in *Amico Serafico* XXXIII, 1, (1948), 1 (see above, Introduction, B). Cf. also C. Lubich, "La comunità cristiana" 2–3.

68. C. Lubich, *Colloqui,* 138 and WRIT-REC February 23, 1971 (Rocca di Papa, Italy, to the gen leaders).

69. *Scr. Sp./2,* 175. Cf. also DIAR February 4, 1962.

70. *Scr. Sp./2,* 187. Cf. also *Meditations,* 77.

71. LET March 6, 1976 (Rocca di Papa, Italy, "Carissimi volontari . . ."). In the same letter she says that "Jesus in our midst" is "the principle of new life in us and of the revolution of love (with all its consequences . . .) around us." In fact, Chiara often speaks of the social revolution that the gospel carries when it is lived (cf. C. Lubich, *Yes, Yes, No, No,* 79; REC March 17, 1975, Frascati, Italy). These passages are not included in this study for they do not mention the specific rapport with Jesus in our midst.

72. LET December 13, 1977 (Rocca di Papa, Italy, "Carissime volontarie . . ."). Cf. also C. Lubich, "Dialogo aperto. Quando i genitori non capiscono" in *Città Nuova,* XX, 22 (1976), 41.

73. REC January 31, 1975 (Rocca di Papa, Italy).

74. *Scr. Sp./1,* 268.

75. C. Lubich, *Colloqui,* 183.

76. C. Lubich, *Meditations,* 81.

77. REC June 8, 1965 (Rocca di Papa, Italy, ecumenical meeting). And REC November 19, 1965 (Liverpool), "If they are two, they already form a cell in their environment, and they try to keep Jesus in their midst, in factories, schools, everywhere."

78. C. Lubich, *Yes, Yes, No, No,* 89–90. In another meditation, entitled "Light a Living Cell," in speaking of Jesus in our midst she says, "In this way you light up a cell of the body of Christ, a living cell, a hearth (*focolare*) of God, whose fire along with its light is communicated to others" (*Ibid.,* 69–72).

79. C. Lubich, *Yes, Yes, No, No,* 87. In speaking also of the great difficulties the future may hold for Christians, Chiara comments in 'Dialogo aperto. La presenza di Gesú fra noi'' in *Città Nuova,* XXII, 1 (1978), 41, "We must not be afraid, for where there are two or more who fully live this phrase of the gospel, Jesus is in their midst. So being, he can enter into factories, schools, homes, everywhere, and render the Church present."

80. C. Lubich, *Colloqui,* 94.

81. *Scr. Sp./1,* 227.

82. C. Lubich, *Diary 1964/65,* 168.

83. C. Lubich, *Yes, Yes, No, No,* 81–82.

84. REC June 3, 1969 (Rocca di Papa, Italy).

85. Cf. REC July 17, 1969 (Grottaferrata, Italy).

86. C. Lubich, "Scuola gen: Chiara risponde" in *Gen,* X, 7 (1976), 1 and REC June 2, 1976 (Grottaferrata, Italy, to the gen school).

87. WRIT 1958 ("Appunti di Regola"), 43–44.

88. DIAR April 22, 1967. Cf. C. Lubich, "L'intelligenza dei santi" in *Gen's,* III, 5 (1975), 1; DIAR May 26, 1971; REC March 17, 1975 (Frascati, Italy, to the priests' school) where she suggests this method for preparing a sermon; and REC December 1, 1975 (Loppiano, Italy, to the international women's music group of the Focolare, Gen Verde) for the composition of a song: "First we must do all our part, as though everything depended on us and our inspiration."

89. See above in Chapter 1, A. "Who is included in the words 'Where two or three'?"

90. C. Lubich, *All One,* 83–84.

91. C. Lubich, *All One,* 84. And REC February 26, 1964 (Grottaferrata, Italy), "We saw all the different social classes, even the ones most in opposition, come together and unite. Above all, we saw a spectacle unfold (produced not by us, but by 'where two or three') . . . (We saw) the Christian community form itself, in a way very similar to the one of the early Christians, where there was the plebeian, the patrician, the rich and the poor, the Roman and the Jew."

92. C. Lubich, *Diary 1964/65,* 94. Cf. also DIAR February 7, 1981.

93. *Scr. Sp./1,* 218. It also says: "The Christian peoples, or their representatives, must know how to immolate their 'collective egos.' This is the price."

94. *Scr. Sp./1,* 164.

95. *Scr. Sp./1,* 164. And *Scr. Sp./2,* 189, "If we will have individual persons who are united in the name of Christ, in the future we will see new peoples."

96. C. Lubich, *Meditations,* 83–84.

Chapter 4. Jesus in Our Midst and the Work of Mary

1. C. Lubich, *Jesus in the Midst*, 16. And REC August 19, 1965 (Ala di Stura, Italy), "Oh, we have Jesus in our midst who forms our walls; he is our sanctuary, we have nothing else."

2. REC August 19, 1965 (Ala di Stura, Italy).

3. C. Lubich, *All One*, 89.

4. REC 1959 (Notes for Mariapolis talks).

5. REC February 26, 1964 (Grottaferrata, Italy). Cf. also REC December 7, 1964 (Nuremberg, Germany, to a group of Evangelical pastors).

6. REC 1959 (Mariapolis preparation 1959). Cf. also REC December 7, 1964 (Nuremberg, Germany, to a group of Evangelical pastors).

7. C. Lubich, *Jesus in the Midst*, 44–45.

8. REC February 26, 1964 (Grottaferrata, Italy). And REC March 21, 1964 (Grottaferrata, Italy), "In general, for what regards the establishment of our rule . . . there is Jesus in our midst, but there is also another element, the role of an instrument, which has been my own part. Thus, the ideas do come to me, but I explain them or expand on them with Jesus in our midst."

9. LET September 23, 1969 (Rocca di Papa, Italy, "Carissimi focolarini . . .").

10. C. Lubich, *All One*, 89. And REC February 26, 1964 (Grottaferrata, Italy), "In those terrible moments we have passed through, and which are still to come, in those moments when everything collapsed around us, who sustained us? Who was our sustainer? Jesus in our midst. Even when tragic moments reached their darkest points, he was still able to repeat to us, 'my yoke is easy and my burden is light.' Why? Because he was in our midst."

11. REC July 7, 1962 (Grottaferrata, Italy).

12. C. Lubich, *All One*, 89–90.

13. REC February 26, 1964 (Grottaferrata, Italy).

14. REC 1959 (Notes for Mariapolis talks).

15. Chiara describes it in REC December 7, 1964 (Nuremberg, Germany, to a group of Evangelical pastors), in this way, "Every so often the Church asked us for a draft of these ideas. Naturally, since we had no priests available in our own circles, and for the fact that we ourselves were not adept in juridical matters, we sought the help of an outside priest. However, this person had not always understood our situation to the full so as to be able to safeguard those ideas suggested by Jesus in our midst. What happened? The Church never approved those rules which were not conforming to what was the work of God. We had no other choice but to submit these rules, and we placed our hope in God. Six different rules were discarded. The seventh one, through a particular circumstance, was written precisely in the way that mirrored what Jesus in our midst had sketched throughout the years. And that was the one which was approved."

16. WRIT July 7, 1962 (Grottaferrata, Italy, "Appunti per il primo discorso sulla Regola").

17. REC August 19, 1960 (Grottaferrata, Italy). And in the same recording, "Each one (of the focolarini who were working there) had their own juridical

147

thoughts . . . but they were all in unity, in harmony; since there was Jesus in our midst, the work went ahead smoothly."

18. *Statuto dei Focolari della Carità (Gli Apostoli dell'Unità)* (Statute of the Focolares of charity [The apostles of unity]) (Trent, 1948), art. 2.

19. See above, Chapter 1, C, "Other comparisons, *f* " and Chapter 2, C.

20. WRIT 1951 ("L'Ordine di Maria e il suo Ideale").

21. Instead, however, we find notes belonging to the same period of another attempted draft, *Costituzioini-Norme: I Focolari dell'Unità* (The constitutions-norms: The Focolares of unity): "The elections are always made by *Jesus in the midst of the electors*. As usual, the basis of mutual charity is established, then after the full communication of each one's thoughts, given with the detachment charity demands, the person is chosen whom everyone holds to be the most suitable."

22. WRIT October 1954 (third rule).

23. WRIT October 1954 (third rule). Cf. also WRIT June 1953, "I Focolari dell'Unità," a typescript presented to Pope Pius XII as a memorandum that illustrates the Focolare's nature and purpose.

24. WRIT 1958 ("Appunti di regola").

25. *Opera di Maria, Statuti* (Rome 1962), 7–8.

26. In commenting on this article, REC September 13, 1966 (Rocca di Papa, Italy), Chiara says, "The characteristic point is really Jesus in our midst, in the sense that God's will for us is to follow Jesus in the collectivity."

27. WRIT 1950 ("Abbozzo di regola").

28. REC July 7, 1962 (Grottaferrata, Italy).

29. DIAR August 15, 1970.

30. DIAR June 3, 1967.

31. REC December 6, 1966 (Loppiano, Italy). And in the same recording, "Therefore it is useless for a Focolarino, a Focolarina, a Volunteer, or a priest to go off to their rooms and sort out personal problems, or say little prayers in order to make headway in the life of charity, if they at first are not already united with Jesus in their midst with their brothers and sisters. The Lord does not listen to these kinds of prayers, they do not arrive at heaven, they do not pierce the heavenly realm—even if they are accompanied by all the sacrifices in the universe, even if the body is put to flames or if all possessions are given to the poor—because the charity St. Paul speaks about is this very charity." Cf. also REC August 19, 1960 (Grottaferrata, Italy).

32. REC September 20, 1966 (Rocca di Papa, Italy).

33. Transcription of a conversation of April 13, 1955 (Milan).

34. Sartori explains, "Every founder is an unrepeatable, charismatic personality, and for this reason would have little meaning or value for the Church. The need lies here to find a way to channel his or her charism so that what is unrepeatable can be made repeatable. The religious institution (or rule) offers this channel." L. Sartori, "Carismi" in *Nuovo Dizionario di Teologia,* ed. G. Barbaglio and S. Dianich (Alba, 1977), 85.

35. For a brief explanation of these branches and sections, cf. G. Lubich, *Intervista al Movimento dei Focolari* (Rome, 1975).

36. C. Lubich, *Colloqui*, 197 and WRIT-REC July 9, 1974 (Rocca di Papa, Italy, to the Gen). And REC September 17, 1961 (Grottaferrata, Italy), "Bearing witness to this is our vocation."

37. WRIT 1958 ("Appunti di Regola, Opera di Maria"), 27. Cf. also WRIT-REC December 25, 1973 (Rocca di Papa, Italy, to the Focolarini).

38. C. Lubich, "Dialogo aperto. Che cos'è il focolare?" in "Città Nuova," XXI, 14 (1977), 41, which contains a portion of an interview made with Chiara by *Rai-TV* (an Italian television station). And REC December 23, 1963 (Grottaferrata, Italy), "The Focolarini have just one task: to offer Christ to the world . . . not so much by means of works of charity, as by means of charity itself, which when reciprocal, offers the presence of Christ in their midst."

39. C. Lubich, *Jesus in the Midst*, 49.

40. C. Lubich, *Jesus in the Midst*, 49. "Besides, what other idea could God have in mind, after sending his son for the salvation of humanity, if not that of rendering in some way possible his presence among human lives so that this presence could remain and continue?" (*Ibid.*).

41. C. Lubich, *Jesus in the Midst*, 51.

42. REC July 19, 1967 (Rocca di Papa, Italy, to a meeting of the married focolarini). Later, REC July 17, 1971 (Rocca di Papa, Italy, once again to meeting of the married focolarini), using the name "family-focolare," she gives a more definite idea. To be called so, the families must have "the *constant* presence of Jesus in their midst" and "the continual witness of Christian life in the family." "In fact" Chiara continues, "a family-focolare can be conceived of only where Jesus in their midst, practically speaking, has solid foundations, just as in any other focolare center."

43. REC September 14, 1960 (Grottaferrata, Italy).

44. WRIT-REC March 28, 1972 (Loppiano, Italy, to the citizens of the permanent Mariapolis).

45. C. Lubich, "Dialogo aperto. Come uscire dall'assurdo di oggi?" in *Città Nuova*, XXI, 1 (1977), 41. About these "little cities" she wrote *in Diary 1964/65*, 103, "And we build our 'Loppianos' like little cities of God, like so many Ars scattered all over the world. Jesus in our midst is the curate, and he must reign there, as was said of the Curate of Ars: 'At Ars Fr. Vianney, "loved like a father," was king.' "

46. C. Lubich, *Jesus in the Midst*, 56.

47. C. Lubich, *Colloqui,* 197, WRIT-REC July 9, 1974 (Rocca di Papa, Italy, to the Gen).

48. REC August 19, 1960 (Grottaferrata, Italy, to the Focolarini).

49. C. Lubich, *All One*, 90. And REC February 26, 1964 (Grottaferrata, Italy), "You know that the rule provides for superiors. . . . Now this superior, which is admitted by the Church, has a particular task. It is to see that the rule is observed. In the rule it is stated that the rule of rules, the norm of every other norm, the premise for every other rule is to put Jesus in our midst."

50. C. Lubich, *All One*, 90. And REC February 26, 1964 (Grottaferrata, Italy), "The superior, when speaking, expresses Jesus in our midst. Who governs in this

case? Jesus. The other is an instrument, who speaks. The superior of this work must be Jesus in our midst, otherwise it is no longer the Work of Mary."

51. C. Lubich, *Diary 1964–65*, 25. Cf. also REC April 24, 1964 (Recife, Brazil).

52. REC June 1, 1969 (Rocca di Papa, Italy). In the same recording Chiara continues, "We are already doing this now . . . you are not aware to what extent things go ahead due to Jesus in our midst." Cf. also REC June 3, 1970 (Rocca di Papa, Italy).

53. WRIT 1951 ("L'Ordine di Maria e il suo Ideale").

54. WRIT 1951 ("L'Ordine di Maria e il suo Ideale"). And DIAR June 9, 1971, "Ours we can often call an enlightened obedience for the fact that, in making ourselves immediately one with the thought of the superior, we put Jesus in our midst, who eventually enlightens the superior on some details that may have escaped him or her or were simply forgotten because we may have set up a wall by the little unity offered on our part."

55. WRIT 1951 ("L'Ordine di Maria e il suo Ideale"). Cf. also REC June 17, 1980 (Loppiano, Italy).

56. DIAR May 23, 1967.

57. REC April 25, 1970 (Rocca di Papa, Italy, to the focolarini).

58. WRIT 1951 ("L'Ordine di Maria e il suo Ideale").

59. WRIT 1951 ("L'Ordine di Maria e il suo Ideale").

60. WRIT 1951 ("L'Ordine di Maria e il suo Ideale"). The following is also interesting for its explanation on obeying "gladly," spoken about above, but from another angle. "The subordinate having the superior within him or herself, senses that the command given is no longer an external command that comes from a human person . . . but it is a command that is felt also deep within. On the other hand, the superior finding him or herself before a subordinate so well disposed and empty of self out of love, will also find the subordinate in him or herself. And if the superior truly loves the subordinate, he or she will give the commands that the divine will wants on that person, interpreted by the superior (because he or she contains the other)" *(ibid)*.

61. WRIT 1951 ("L'Ordine di Maria e il suo Ideale").

62. WRIT 1962 (?) ("E nacque il Focolare . . .").

63. LET September 6, 1947 (Fiera di Primiero, Italy, "Carissima C. e compagne . . ."). See also above, Introduction, B.

64. WRIT 1947 (Osimo, Italy), shown here in the form adapted for a prepared text to be read, WRIT-REC December 7, 1972 (Rocca di Papa, Italy). And REC August 20, 1965 (Ala di Stura, Italy), "It is she who helps us grow in this presence of Jesus in our midst, which is our everything."

65. C. Lubich, "Chiara risponde," in *Movimento dei Focolari: notiziario interno*, (June 1975), 1–2 and REC March 17, 1975 (Frascati, Italy). And REC January 31, 1969 (Rocca di Papa, Italy, to the priests), "What does Jesus in our midst mean? It means having this function: we miserable creatures are able, in a marian way, to give Christ to the world, not physically, but spiritually, if we love one another to the point of being ready to die for one another." Cf. also

S. De Fiores, *Maria presenza viva nel popolo di Dio* (Rome, 1980), 18, 226, 233, where the author underlines this aspect of the Focolare: "to live Mary" by generating Jesus in our midst.

66. REC November 19, 1965 (Liverpool, to a group of Anglicans).

67. REC November 19, 1965 (Liverpool, to a group of Anglicans).

68. WRIT 1962 (?) ("E nacque il Focolare . . ."). Cf. also WRIT June 16, 1978 ("Una spiritualità per il laicato d'oggi"). And REC March 25, 1962 (Grottaferrata, Italy), "He made me clearly see Mary as the model of our spirituality, she who lives this spirituality of the Mystical Body. In fact, it is she who expresses the Mystical Body, she who is mother, she who is unity."

69. C. Lubich, "L'ideale dell'unità," in *Città Nuova,* XXII, 13 (1978), 40.

70. C. Lubich, *All One,* 52. And REC November 19, 1963 (Grottaferrata, Italy), "In our efforts in building the Work of Mary as we journeyed ahead, we often times had the distinct impression that we were building Mary."

71. WRIT April 3, 1974 ("Leggendo uno scritto di don Alberione"), recorded on videotape. Cf. also DIAR February 7, 1981.

72. WRIT-REC December 25, 1972 (Rocca di Papa, Italy, to the focolarini).

73. REC February 26, 1964 (Grottaferrata, Italy). Cf. also REC August 13, 1963 (Ala di Stura, Italy, to a group of children); REC December 7, 1964 (Nuremberg, Germany, to a group of Evangelical pastors).

74. DIAR June 3, 1967.

Glossary

Focolare:　　　An Italian word meaning "hearth" or "family fireside." It was the name given to the initial group by others who felt the "warmth" of their love. Focolare refers to the movement as a whole, also known as the Work of Mary.

Focolare center:　A small community of either men or women, who have vows of poverty, chastity and obedience, whose first aim is to achieve among themselves the unity Jesus prayed for, through the practice of mutual love. There are also married members who live with their families.

Focolarina:　　A member of a women's focolare center, plural—Focolarine.

Focolarino:　　A member of a men's focolare center, plural—Focolarini (also used to indicate focolarine and focolarini collectively).

Gen:　　　　　Meaning New *Gen*eration, refers to the members of a youth branch of the Focolare.

Ideal:　　　　The word Ideal is used in the Focolare primarily to mean God, chosen as the one aim in life. Secondly it also stands for the Focolare spirituality and the way it is lived in daily life.

Mariapolis:　　A summer meeting of persons of all vocations, ages, and social classes whose sole purpose is to live the experience of reciprocal love.

Order of Mary:　A name attributed to the Focolare in its early days.

**Permanent
Mariapolis:**　　"Little cities" whose purpose is the same as the summer Mariapolises. The first permanent Mariapolis is situated near Florence, in a locality called "Loppiano." Presently there are thirteen others around the world including Mariapolis Luminosa in Hyde Park, New York.

Volunteers: Lay persons who want to respond to the totalitarian call of giving themselves to God according to the spirituality of the Work of Mary, while remaining in the world. They meet regularly in small groups called "nuclei."

Works by Chiara Lubich Available in English

A CALL TO LOVE

Spiritual Writings, Vol. 1

"Chiara Lubich has established herself as a Christian writer of considerable proportions. Given her prolific literary output it is fitting that New City Press should issue a retrospective series of Lubich's best works, titled Spiritual Writings. The first work in this series *A Call to Love* comprises three of her most popular studies of momentous Christian living: *Our Yes to God* (1980), *The Word of Life* (1974), and *The Eucharist* (1977)."

B.C. Catholic

ISBN 0-911782-70-2, paper, 5 1/8 x 8, 180 pp.

WHEN OUR LOVE IS CHARITY

Spiritual Writings, Vol. 2

Since publishing her first book in 1959, Chiara Lubich has written extensively on a variety of spiritual topics drawn from the gospel message of unity. This second volume of spiritual writings binds together three of her previous works: *Charity, Jesus in Our Midst*, and *When Did We See You, Lord?*

ISBN 0-911782-93-1, paper, 5 1/8 x 8, 152 pp.

UNITY AND JESUS FORSAKEN

"Without being simplistic or reductionistic, Lubich challenges [the reader] to focus on Jesus forsaken as the

model for unity and the key to living a life of joy. . . .
Lubich's essays reflect a balanced spirituality."

FROM SCRIPTURE TO LIFE

"Contains commentaries that author Chiara Lubich has written on 12 different 'Words of Life.' Each section of the book includes true stories of people who applied the teaching of the Scripture passage."

MEDITATIONS

"[A] collection of brief but intensely meaningful thoughts carefully mined from the scriptures. Chiara helps us to see all the events of our lives as opportunities for our ultimate . . . perfection."

ON THE HOLY JOURNEY

"Every two weeks, Chiara Lubich, foundress and president of the Focolare movement, sends out a spiritual message to committed members throughout the world. This is a collection of those meditations, the principal focus of which is a call to live out the 'holy journey' toward Christian perfection in the world by 'walking together' in the love of Jesus and Mary."

DIARY 1964/65

"Add Chiara Lubich's name to the list of extraordinary Catholic women. . . . In 1964 and 1965 Chiara Lubich made several trips to North and South America to encourage the Focolarini who were establishing their work in the U.S., Argentina, and Brazil. Lubich's diary records her experiences and thoughts during these journeys."

New Oxford Review

ISBN 0-911782-55-9, paper, 5 1/8 x 8, 188 pp.

Works on Chiara Lubich and the Focolare Movement

UNITY—OUR ADVENTURE

The Focolare Movement

This publication tells the story of an adventure: that of the Focolare movement. The book intends to offer a quick panorama of the Focolare's spirituality and history. It contains 40 color and 47 black and white photos.

ISBN 0-911782-56-7, cloth, 8 1/2 x 11, 80 pp.

STARS AND TEARS

by Michel Pochet

Through a series of interviews with Chiara Lubich, the author traces the development and the spirituality of the Focolare. The style and format is accessible to everyone.

ISBN 0-911782-54-0, paper, 5 1/8 x 8, 153 pp.

GOD WHO IS LOVE

In the Experience and Thought of Chiara Lubich

by Marisa Cerini

A spiritual-dogmatic study that begins to uncover the rich wisdom and theological doctrine found in the thoughts and writings of Chiara Lubich. The reality of God as love in her experience shows itself as something authentically new, while following the rich tradition of the Church.

ISBN 1-56548-004-X, paper, 5 1/8 x 8, 96 pp.